# COIN COLLECTING 101

## THE ONLY BEGINNER'S GUIDE YOU'LL EVER NEED TO BUILD, IDENTIFY, PRESERVE, AND CASH IN ON YOUR COIN COLLECTION

## THOMAS KNOLLS

# CONTENTS

# INTRODUCTION

In the hushed corners of my family's history, a story unfolds— one that transports me back to the harrowing days of the early 1860s.

My great-grandfather's service and experience as a soldier in the American Civil War are still fresh in my mind. Amidst the intensity of battle, he uncovered a remarkable artifact—a pine tree shilling. This coin displayed Latin inscriptions, Roman numerals denoting the year 1652, and, on the flip side, a striking depiction of a pine tree accompanied by the word "Massachusetts."

He had passed the coin down to my grandfather, who kept it locked away in his safe and only broke out his treasure once per year—on Thanksgiving day. As a young boy, I listened attentively to my grandfather's tale about his father, which never ceased to captivate my imagination. It was in those days that my enduring passion for numismatics, the study of coins, was cultivated.

In July 2023, I read about a cache of over 700 gold coins discovered in a Kentucky cornfield earlier in the year. Believed to have been buried to protect against Confederate raiders during the Civil War, the coins date back to the years between 1840 and 1863 (Solly, 2023).

They include $10 gold coins featuring Lady Liberty, rare $20 gold Liberty double eagles minted in 1863, and $1 coins referred to as Indian princess dollars. Given the coins' federal origin, it's plausible that the stash's owner had dealings with the federal government, prompting caution against potential Confederate raids.

The cache carries an estimated value of $2 million. It contains a notable collection of Civil War-era coinage, including pieces from the Dahlonega Mint—a discovery of significant historical and numismatic status (Solly, 2023). Like the Charlotte Mint, the Dahlonega Mint also fell under Confederate control during the Civil War. Due to the limited production of coins at the Dahlonega Mint, all of its coins are considered scarce and hold significant value.

The unearthing in 2023 triggered a flood of childhood recollections and memories of my personal coin discoveries throughout the years and sparked the flame to write this book.

This book is intended to provide a comprehensive guide for people new to numismatics. The core aim is to give readers the essential information and tools to begin a rewarding voyage into coin collecting.

Numismatology is more than just an intriguing pastime; it's also an extremely profitable enterprise. Those who acquire and trade coins often do so for three reasons: to gain knowledge, to pursue investment possibilities, and to indulge their passions.

- **Knowledge and expertise:** For those entering the realm of coin collecting, the thirst for knowledge goes beyond merely amassing physical relics. Aspiring collectors are eager to uncover the rich tapestry of history woven into each coin, tracing their origins, understanding the different types and designs, and deciphering the subtle intricacies of valuation. The aspiration is not just to hold coins but to wield the expertise that enables informed decisions—a mastery that transforms collecting from a casual pursuit into a scholarly endeavor.
- **Investment and profit:** Beyond the allure of history and aesthetics, coin collecting offers an avenue for potential financial gain. Beginners often recognize that their acquisitions could appreciate over time. This financial perspective introduces an element of strategic thinking. Enthusiasts are keen to learn the secrets of identifying coins with intrinsic and market value and discovering the nuances that elevate a coin's worth. Insights into these aspects allow newcomers to not only enjoy the aesthetics of their collection but also view it as a form of investment with profit potential.

- **Exploration and passion:** Numismatics isn't merely about assembling a set of coins—it's an exploration of human history, culture, and artistry. Some individuals are drawn to coin collecting by an innate curiosity about the stories behind each coin, be it a coin from ancient times or a minting from a critical period in modern history. This journey of exploration becomes a passionate pursuit, where the simple act of holding a coin becomes a bridge to the past. Numismatic intrigue can develop into an all-consuming passion, transforming collecting from a casual hobby into a lifelong obsession.

This book takes you on a fascinating trip into the world of coin collecting, delving deep into the emotional and historical aspects that coins carry. These stories engage and resonate with us by connecting us to a bygone era.

You will unearth a treasure trove of coin types, inviting you to explore ancient and historical coins, commemorative pieces, and the world of investment opportunities. Some of you might be cautious about promising investments that turn out to be fraudulent or Ponzi schemes. This book was created to help you recognize legitimate investment prospects and detect scammers from a mile away.

As our adventure continues, we unveil the hidden historical narratives that coins carry. They're like little windows into history, allowing us a glance into significant discoveries as we gain fresh perspectives on the past's mysteries. Now, imagine the same coins as historical keepsakes and potential financial assets. This guide sheds light on how coins hold both roles—making them not only fascinating but potentially valuable.

Switching tools, you'll dig deeper into coin grading and valuation—breaking down why they matter and giving you a sneak peek into the process. We want you to feel equipped with the tools to assess coin quality and understand their worth. And speaking of tools, have you ever wondered about the thrill of hunting for coins?

We'll unveil the excitement, tools, and stories behind the art of uncovering hidden numismatic treasures. Consider this book your reliable partner, meticulously designed to lead you from a novice with a fascination for coins to a well-versed collector equipped with the wisdom and abilities needed to assemble a collection that authentically reflects your enthusiasm and mastery.

Our adventure takes another twist as we head into the world of rare and unusual coins. Imagine discovering legends, mysteries, and anomalies that leave collectors awe-struck. We'll share stories of legendary finds, delve into the fascination of error coins, and explore the intriguing world of pattern and trial coins. These are the kind of stories that'll pique your curiosity and make you want to travel a little deeper.

Now, imagine coins not just as pieces of metal but as intricate works of art. The evolution of coin design explores the stories they tell through symbols and images. It's like uncovering the secrets artists and history have hidden in plain sight.

We'll navigate authenticity, cultural sensitivity, and environmental responsibility in the coin-collecting sphere. These are the values that guide our interactions within the numismatic community. It's about showing respect, making fair deals, and leaving a positive impact.

Finally, this book concludes by celebrating the legends of the coin-collecting world. Imagine meeting collectors who've left a mark on history—those who've shaped the hobby and inspired others. Their accounts are beyond mere fairytales; they are future blueprints, leading the next generation of collectors.

This is undoubtedly the ONLY beginner's guide you will ever need to build, identify, preserve, and cash in on your very own coin collection.

# 1

# THE ALLURE OF COIN COLLECTING

In the heart of the untamed woods, during my adventurous teenage years in the Boy Scouts, I stumbled upon more than just the beauty of nature; I found a coin that would change the course of my life, a coin with a story as valuable as glittering gold.

It was a coin unlike any I had ever seen. Its edges were worn, and its surface bore the scars of time, but it still held an undeniable allure. The image of Lady Liberty graced one side, her majestic profile a testament to a bygone era. On the reverse, a braided hair half cent from the year 1850 stared back at me, surrounded by a wreath of leaves.

At that moment, amidst the solitude of the forest and the soft rustling of leaves, I felt an inexplicable connection to the coin. It was as if I had stumbled upon a tangible piece of history, a small but significant relic that had weathered the ages.

My heart raced with curiosity and wonder. Who owned this coin, and how did it come to rest here, far from any human settlement? The forest seemed to hold secrets, and this coin was a tantalizing clue to a story waiting to be unearthed.

Little did I know that this happenstance finding would be the final catalyst for a lifelong fascination with coin collecting. This passion would lead me to unravel the hidden mysteries behind every coin and appreciate the rich history connected to these small, unassuming pieces of metal.

## WHAT IS NUMISMATICS?

Numismatics, the intricate study of physical representations of currency, takes us on a journey beyond the mere coins in our pockets. It reveals a world where coins are not just tokens of trade; they are storytellers.

Before the 19th century, coin collecting was a personal pursuit reserved for the elite, religious leaders, and rulers (Kelly, 2022). Even emperors like Caesar Augustus were avid collectors, using coins for trade negotiations and as goodwill gestures.

Ancient coins held a unique allure in stark contrast to today's familiar quarters, nickels, dimes, and pennies. The first ancient coins hailed from the Far East, crafted meticulously from precious metals like gold and silver. Later, the Persians introduced copper and bronze coins of varying weights and values.

Each dynasty's creations were distinct in the world of ancient Chinese coins. The oldest surviving Chinese coins, dating back to 610 AD, often emerge from tombs as the treasured possessions of the deceased (APMEX, 2022). Unlike the rounded forms elsewhere, these coins came in striking shapes like seashells or spades.

The Romans were trailblazers in standardizing currency, minting didrachms from silver in 280 BC (APMEX, 2022). They also crafted bronze coins, which are highly sought after by collectors. This standardization aimed to ensure fair trade, marking a shift towards currency exchange for goods and services.

On the other hand, Ancient Greek coins initially bore detailed animal imagery stamped with geometric patterns. Over time, they evolved to showcase human faces on gold coins, incorporating various metals like bronze. The drachm served as the fundamental unit of currency, its values meticulously calibrated to facilitate transactions, from purchasing livestock to determining wages.

Gold coins, cherished for their inherent value, emerged from various corners of the world. During the 7th century BC, the Persian Empire held a significant share of the world's gold, while North Africa gained renown for its abundant gold deposits and production of gold coins (APMEX, 2022).

Numismatics is not just about collecting coins; it is a gateway to exploring history and culture. Each coin carries a distinctive narrative, offering glimpses into the era, the people, and the events of its time. Collectors unearth stories from diverse societies, political regimes, and pivotal moments. Coins provide tangible links to the past, allowing collectors to appreciate and learn from the rich history of human civilization.

So, whether you are on the quest for ancient Greek coins or other relics from the past, understanding the pivotal role of coins in shaping commerce enriches your collection. In a world dominated by paper money, coins endure as tangible relics. Archaeologists continue to uncover ancient artifacts, bearing witness to the craftsmanship of bygone eras. Embrace coin collecting as your passport to a captivating world of history, culture, and the tangible stories each coin carries.

## EVOLUTION OF COIN COLLECTING

The journey of coin collecting, driven by aesthetics rather than just bullion value, has a rich history that has evolved over the centuries. It gained popularity during the European Renaissance of the 14th century when society embraced a renewed interest in the past and sought to explore all aspects of life. Coin collecting gradually transitioned from a royal pastime to a hobby for the financially privileged.

The Enlightenment period that succeeded the Renaissance witnessed the rise of industrialization and the emergence of the middle class, a crucial part of the national economy. However, lacking the historical heritage of royalty, the middle class sought to emulate royal practices, including the hobby of coin collection.

Today, coin collecting has become a well-developed hobby accessible to specialized collectors and those with budget constraints.

Now, you might wonder: Why invest in coin collecting, both financially and in terms of time? Here are some reasons why:

- **The beauty of imperfections:** In coin collecting, imperfections and printing errors take center stage, carrying significant value. Occasionally, mints release coins with mistakes, some visible and others nearly imperceptible. In exceptionally rare instances, these errors are glaring, like a coin devoid of any distinct imprint or one bearing the same mark on both sides. While the ideal scenario is to catch and rectify these errors at the mint, a handful inevitably slips into the market, becoming the coveted white whales for collectors who eagerly hunt them down. Conversely, more conventional collectors aim to satiate their appetites by seeking the pinnacle of perfection in coins. However, this pursuit of flawlessness is a relative concept, influenced by diverse factors such as the coin's date and place of manufacture, as well as its shape, weight, and size compared to other specimens.
- **It's an educational experience:** Collecting coins offers a multifaceted educational experience. It delves into cultural and historical exploration, revealing insights into political trends and a nation's economic development. Examining changes in coin weight over time provides a tangible understanding of currency devaluation due to global inflation. For instance, comparing a current Indian 5-rupee coin with one minted two decades ago showcases this difference. Similarly, the disappearance of smaller denominations

due to inflation, like the Indian 25-paisa coin, underscores these monetary shifts. Coin collecting, therefore, serves as a comprehensive education encompassing cultural studies, economics, and politics for enthusiastic collectors.

- **Coins offer financial benefits:** Investing in a coin collection can be a smart financial move. Rare coins often contain precious metals, and their value tends to rise due to global inflation. Factors like manufacturing details, special issuances, and printing errors also play a role in coin valuation. This combination of factors makes coin collections a potentially lucrative investment, with the potential for higher returns when selling or auctioning the collection (Seth, 2016).

In essence, coin collecting is a pursuit that not only holds potential financial rewards but also provides an engaging and enlightening journey through history, culture, and the nuances of human civilization.

## THE ART OF NUMISMATIC CLASSIFICATION

Let us dive into coin grading. It's an intricate puzzle where opinions can differ, and there's no one-size-fits-all scientific scale to rely on. To make things even more interesting, each country has its lingo for describing coin grades, adding a layer of complexity.

Disagreements about grading have been around since day one and will likely continue. But fear not; there is some common ground among coin collectors and dealers regarding grading, even though it can be a hot topic in numismatics.

Think of coin grading as an art form. It demands an eagle eye and years of scrutinizing countless coins. As collectors gain experience, they often specialize in specific types or eras of coins, each with its own set of grading standards.

Coins get their grades based on factors like when and where they were made and what materials were used (*A Comprehensive*, n.d.). But here's the catch: Grading is subjective, and opinions vary. No universally accepted scientific scale exists.

Professional numismatists usually specialize in particular types or historical periods of coins, and each group has its own grading rules. Take the NGC (Numismatic Guaranty Corporation), for example. They have a detailed grading system. When collectors send coins to the NGC, they get carefully documented, barcoded, and safely stored until the NGC's coin graders get to work (*The NGC*, n.d.). Before grading, coins that might have specific designations are examined by specialists who know all about those details. Every coin is compared to published references to see if it fits one particular category.

While a coin's grade is part of what determines its value, there are other factors to consider, like how rare it is, its condition, and how much collectors want it. This book aims to provide you with a detailed introduction to the art of coin grading. However, it's wise to consult a professional numismatist or appraiser to assess a coin's worth accurately. They will consider all these elements, giving you a clearer picture of your coin's value.

## EXPLORING DIFFERENT COIN CATEGORIES

Have you ever pondered the allure of coins, those small metallic discs that have silently shaped our world? From ancient civilizations to our modern societies, these unassuming treasures have woven a remarkable tapestry of history, culture, and artistry. Their enduring value and the enchanting stories they carry await your discovery.

For those enchanted by their allure, numismatics is a passionate pursuit. It beckons enthusiasts who appreciate these tiny treasures' artistry, historical significance, and diverse beauty. As a collector, you will find immense joy in assembling a collection that may span from the ancient Greek drachmas to the rare commemorative coins of our contemporary world. Numismatics also offers a unique window into economic trends, reflecting the prosperity, political stability, and cultural evolution of different eras. Beyond that, collecting coins is a fascinating educational journey, offering insights into geography, mythology, and the artistic expressions of various civilizations.

What truly distinguishes coins is their remarkable ability to encapsulate stories and memorialize historical events. Each coin carries the legacy of its time, preserving images and inscriptions that illuminate essential milestones. Whether it's the Roman denarius witnessing the conquests of Julius Caesar or American coins proudly featuring iconic figures like George Washington and Abraham Lincoln, these small disks narrate tales of triumph, defeat, and the ever-changing course of societies.

With their historical richness and timeless appeal, coins continue to hold us in awe. These modest artifacts connect to the past, offering glimpses into the vibrant cultures and civilizations that preceded our time. From the early Lydian coins, bearing witness to the dawn of coinage, to the intricacies of modern minting, coins stand as invaluable relics of human ingenuity. They patiently reside in our pockets, awaiting our curiosity to unlock the fascinating narratives concealed within.

# 2

# LAYING THE FOUNDATIONS— TYPES OF COINS TO COLLECT

D id you know there are more currencies in the world than recognized languages? There are 195 recognized countries today, and each one has its own coins, some with designs that would leave you in awe—waiting to be discovered by avid collectors like you.

From ancient civilizations' elaborate patterns to today's contemporary minting wonders, the world of coin collecting is a treasure trove of history, culture, and artistry begging to be explored. If you have ever held a piece of history in your hand, you will know how it feels to grasp a tiny artifact with a unique story that transcends time and place.

Imagine traveling through time and geography with each coin you collect, discovering the tales of emperors and leaders, the symbols of nations, and the evolution of currency itself. From Roman denarii to Indian rupees, American eagles to Chinese pandas, each coin carries a piece of our shared human history puzzle.

## COMMEMORATIVE AND SPECIAL ISSUE COINS

You may or may not have paused to ponder the world of commemorative coins. These extraordinary tokens, minted to honor pivotal events, notable figures, or significant anniversaries in a nation's history, possess a captivating history and enduring allure.

This section showcases the art and significance of these unique coins, exploring their artistic, historical, cultural, economic, and educational values, all contributing to their central role in the mesmerizing field of numismatics.

Commemorative coins are more than mere metal; they are miniature masterpieces. Crafting these coins is an intricate art form, often featuring detailed portraits of historical figures, vivid depictions of momentous events, and renditions of iconic landmarks. Consider the U.S. Bicentennial quarters, vividly capturing Paul Revere's midnight ride and a patriotic drummer boy. The artistry behind these coins forms a tangible connection to the events or people they honor, elevating them far beyond mere currency.

Beyond their artistic beauty, commemorative coins hold cultural and historical significance. They serve as miniature time capsules, encapsulating significant historical moments and embodying cultural values and national pride. Take, for example, the French Sower Silver coin, symbolizing the enduring strength of the French Republic. Similarly, India's 75th Independence Day commemorative coin reflects a nation's pride and journey forward (*The Art*, 2023). These coins are invaluable cultural artifacts, narrating rich stories of our shared human history.

Material composition, scarcity, age, and desirability do not solely determine the economic value of coins within the coin collector community. Rare specimens like the 1936 Canadian Dot Cent are highly coveted and command astonishing prices at auctions. However, their true worth extends beyond monetary value, residing in their historical and cultural significance.

Commemorative coins also serve as powerful educational tools, fostering a deeper understanding of history and culture. Numerous educational programs leverage these coins to inspire learning. For instance, the Royal Canadian Mint's *Coins of Canada* program encourages young Canadians to explore their nation's rich history through coin collecting (*The Art*, 2023).

Crafting a commemorative coin is meticulous, from the initial concept to the final product. The minting process showcases exceptional craftsmanship, with each coin carefully engraved and stamped. Esteemed institutions like the U.S. Mint and the Royal Mint are responsible for issuing these coins, ensuring their quality and authenticity.

Within the world of numismatics, commemorative coins occupy a special place. They frequently become the crown jewels of collections due to their historical and artistic significance. Distinguished numismatists, including the esteemed Q.

David Bowers, hold a particular fascination for these coins, as each tells a distinct story.

Commemorative coins transcend the metal they are crafted from; they are works of art, historical chronicles, cultural symbols, economic assets, and educational tools—all woven into one. They enrich the enchanting domain of numismatics, allowing everyone to hold a tangible fragment of history.

## BULLION AND INVESTMENT COINS

Let us delve deeper into bullion coins, which are valuable because they consist of precious metals like gold, silver, and platinum. Interestingly, they come in different weights, typically fractions of one troy ounce (a medieval French measure for precious metals, equals 31.103 grams, per the U.K. Royal Mint) (Chen, 2023).

Numerous nations issue official bullion coins. You may have heard of the United States Mint's American Eagle series or the Royal Canadian Mint's Canadian Maple Leaf series. These coins are not just for collectors; some buy them as investments, seeing them as a way to protect their money from inflation.

The value of these precious metal coins depends on a few things. First, the coin's intrinsic value is all about the precious metal it contains. Then, you've got the mintage value, which is how many of these coins are in the market. Of course, demand for the coin is also a big player in its value. Furthermore, let's not forget about the condition and grade of the coin—that can make a real difference.

Now, here is where it gets interesting. When investing in coins, you must find that sweet spot between your love for collecting and your investment strategy. A well-rounded portfolio should have different types of coins to balance things out and reduce risks. It is crucial to do your homework and research before you start buying, and also think about where you will keep these precious metals once you've got them.

Investing in coins can be a wise fiscal decision, especially when diversifying your portfolio and safeguarding your finances against economic ups and downs. Just remember, risks are involved like any investment, so it's good to stay informed and make choices that work for you.

## UNRAVELING THE MYSTERIES OF MINT MARKS AND ENGRAVINGS

In numismatics, the little details can make all the difference, and that is certainly the case regarding mintmarks. These tiny letters on coins might seem insignificant, but they hold a wealth of information and significance for coin collectors.

First and foremost, mintmarks help collectors in their quest to acquire coins from every possible date and mintmark combination within a series. You must know your mintmarks inside and out if you are serious about collecting. They can be a major factor in determining a coin's rarity and value, but they are also like little windows into the fascinating history of American coinage.

You see, it all started in 1792 when the first U.S. Mint fired up its operations in Philadelphia, the nation's capital at the time (Sanders, 2021). Later on, in 1838, three branch mints joined the game: Charlotte in North Carolina, Dahlonega in Georgia (thanks to some nearby gold discoveries), and New Orleans to support the booming commerce in the South. These branches had their own unique production patterns.

When the nation expanded westward, new mints popped up accordingly. The government created the San Francisco Mint in 1854 due to the California Gold Rush. Silver mining in the western states prompted the minting of coins in Carson City, Nevada, from 1870 to 1893. Then, Denver, Colorado, got in on the action in 1906 (Sanders, 2021).

Each mint had its style and specialties. In the 19th century, as the main mint, Philadelphia cranked out gold, silver, copper, and copper-nickel coins. New Orleans was known for its silver production, while San Francisco struck plenty of gold and silver coins. Carson City had a smaller output, mostly silver, and Charlotte and Dahlonega produced only gold coins.

Fast forward to the early 20th century, and most circulating coins came from Philadelphia and Denver. In 1974, a minting facility was set up in West Point, New York. More recently, West Point and the San Francisco Mint have mainly produced collector coins.

Usually, you can tell which mint made a coin pretty quickly. Older Philadelphia coins typically do not have a mintmark, except for nickels struck in 1942-45, which have a "P." Starting in 1979, Philadelphia dollars were marked as such. Since 1980, all coins made there (except cents) have a mintmark (Sanders, 2021).

Branch mint coins have different mintmarks: Charlotte (C), Carson City (CC), Dahlonega (D), Denver (D), New Orleans (O), San Francisco (S), and West Point (W). Despite Dahlonega and Denver using a "D," there's not much confusion since the Georgia Mint only existed from 1838 to 1861, while the Colorado Mint started in the 20th century (Sanders, 2021).

But here's where it gets tricky. Sometimes, you can't pinpoint the mint, especially during certain times. In the mid-1960s, mints hid their marks due to fears of collectors hoarding coins. In the '70s and '80s, circulating coins from San Francisco and West Point were made without mintmarks.

Mintmarks can also change positions within a coin series. Before 1965, they usually appeared on the reverse (tails) side, but after that, they moved to the obverse (heads). Coins are typically listed in date-mintmark format, like "1989" for no mintmark and "1989-D" for Denver.

The bottom line is that mintmarks can turn a common coin into something extraordinary. Take the 1916 Mercury dime, for example. Over 20 million were struck in Philadelphia and more than 10 million in San Francisco, but just 264,000 came out of Denver. That is why the 1916-D is scarce and valuable compared to the more common 1916 and 1916-S (Sanders, 2021).

As a numismatist, understanding mintmarks is essential for collecting American coins. They are like your secret decoder ring for collecting coins and uncovering their origins. A coin's rarity, value, and history are often closely tied to where it was minted, and that's why mintmarks are a vital part of your coin-collecting journey.

## ENGRAVED ARTISTRY

The journey from concept to coin is fascinating, and engraving plays a pivotal role. In the early years of the United States Mint, engraving was a labor-intensive task, often done by hand at the actual coin size. However, as the 20th century rolled in, the process evolved.

Artists began working on larger models, around 12 inches in diameter, which they could then scale down to coin size. This innovation opened the door to collaborations with talented outside artists like Augustus Saint-Gaudens, James Earle Fraser, and Adolph Weinman, who went on to create iconic American coinage (Sanders, 2022).

The journey to creating a coin design typically started with initial models made of clay, followed by versions in plaster or similar materials. From there, a metal rendition known as a galvano was crafted. This galvano was then meticulously scaled down to coin size using a pantograph. One stylus would trace every detail of the model while another simultaneously copied the miniature design onto steel. It was a wholly physical process, a true labor of artistry and precision.

In modernity, the entire engraving process has undergone a remarkable transformation thanks to digital technology. If you have seen a recent animated film, you know that representing three-dimensional objects in a two-dimensional format can be incredibly realistic. In fact, the technology of animated movies introduced digital innovation to the United States Mint, all thanks to Chief Engraver John Mercanti's experience watching *Shrek* with his grandson (Sanders, 2022).

Contemporary engraving is now executed through advanced digital means, employing hardware and software. This technology not only mimics the art of physical sculpting but also expands artistic possibilities. The process begins with an input device resembling a pen attached to a stylus arm, offering force feedback that feels like sculpting with clay. The results are immediately displayed on a large, high-resolution screen, allowing the artist to view and enlarge the image from any angle.

This digital approach brings several advantages. Artists can now seamlessly incorporate modifications and fixes into a virtual medium, a far cry from the challenges of altering a physical model. Standard templates for elements like lettering and dates can be easily integrated. Moreover, this modern method respects tradition, as a three-dimensional scanner can capture the nuances of a physical model. This is especially beneficial for artists who prefer to work with clay and recreate historical patterns.

The pinnacle of the engraving process arrives with the production of dies for coinage. Coins and medals undergo a distinctive technique of not being etched but instead shaped through pressing. To bestow a design upon these items, the Mint relies on a specialized tool, a die, which exerts a forceful impression. Another essential component comes into play for the creation of the die: the hub stamp. This hub stamp displays a positive image in contrast to the die, which bears the image in reverse. Digital becomes physical through a computerized numerical cutting (CNC) process known for its extraordinary precision (Sanders, 2022). These master dies, in turn, give birth to the working dies used in coin production.

For over 2,500 years, dies have been meeting metal to craft coins (Sanders, 2022). The traditional process of making dies in coinage involved engraving the design by hand onto a piece of metal, typically steel or iron. Engravers, skilled artisans, painstakingly carved the intricate design onto the die using specialized tools and techniques. This manual engraving process was labor-intensive and required exceptional craftsmanship. With the integration of digital technology, this age-old process has been ushered into a new millennium, combining artistry with cutting-edge precision.

## VARIATIONS IN DESIGN AND HIDDEN DETAILS

Now, we enter the captivating world of coin design, where every mint, year, and denomination brings a unique visual story. Take the United States Mint, for instance, which churns out billions of coins annually (Meredith, 2020). Some find their way into everyday transactions, while others are crafted exclusively for collectors.

Bringing these designs to life is a meticulous journey involving multiple intricate steps. It begins with legislation, where the fate of a coin's look and feel takes shape. Stakeholder input plays a vital role, ensuring the consideration of diverse perspectives. Artists conduct extensive study and submit design entries to convey the spirit of the subject matter. The legal review ensures compliance with all relevant regulations, followed by artistic improvements and coinability checks to verify that form and function align seamlessly. Finally, committee review adds the finishing touches, ensuring the design is nothing short of exceptional (Meredith, 2020).

That being said, the subtleties of design extend beyond aesthetics. They can significantly impact a coin's value. Consider the Royal Canadian Mint, which pioneered the Bullion Coin DNA system (James, 2020). This innovative approach embeds encrypted image codes directly onto the coins, linking them to a secure RCM database. These advanced security features authenticate the coins and enhance their desirability and worth.

Beyond security, coin designs can harbor hidden gems, like micro-engravings and Easter eggs. These concealed elements add an extra layer of fascination to coin collecting. Take, for example, the Royal Canadian Mint's "Laser Mark Micro Engraving" privy marks and intricate laser-engraved radial lines etched into the fields of their coins (James, 2020). These intricacies serve not only as aesthetic enhancements but also as additional layers of security.

Discovering these concealed details becomes a rewarding adventure for coin collectors, elevating the joy of this beloved hobby. Coin design is a realm where artistry meets technology, every detail holds significance, and the stories within each coin unfold in fascinating ways.

## CASE STUDY: FROM HOBBYIST TO SUCCESSFUL COLLECTOR

For some fortunate individuals, a bank is not just a place to deposit or borrow money; it's a treasure trove waiting to be unlocked through the captivating hobby of *coin roll hunting*. This pursuit involves bringing home rolls of coins from banks and sifting through them in search of valuable coins worth more than their face value. The allure of this hobby has drawn thousands of enthusiasts, and the rewards can be astonishing.

The journey into coin roll hunting often begins with a curious discovery, as in the case of Megan Green from Texas. She stumbled upon a YouTube video showcasing a 1970 Washington quarter valued at $35,000 due to a rare mint error. Intrigued by the idea, she decided to give this new hobby a shot, hoping it could be both enjoyable and financially beneficial (Zetlin, 2019).

Starting her coin roll hunting adventure with a $25 face-value package comprising 50 penny rolls, Green persevered, gradually expanding her efforts. After months of dedication, her persistence paid off when she unearthed a 1969-S Doubled Die Obverse penny—a true treasure among coin collectors. In numismatics, a "double die" refers to a coin that exhibits doubling in some or all of its design elements–a result of an error that occurs during the coin's minting process.

Collectors often find double-die coins intriguing and valuable because of their rarity and uniqueness. The 1969-S Lincoln cent is known for being the canvas of one of the most sought-after and rarest doubled die varieties in numismatics. Her discovery, authenticated by the Professional Coin Grading Service, was valued at an impressive $24,000, with the potential to fetch even higher prices.

Coin roll hunting offers financial potential and the thrill of uncovering hidden gems. The best part? It's a cost-effective hobby that requires little more than time, effort, and a magnifying glass. If you are considering joining this fascinating pursuit, here are some expert tips to get you started:

- **Patience is key:** Coin roll hunting can be both rewarding and frustrating. Expect periods of limited success, but stay persistent in your quest. The thrill of discovery and the potential financial rewards make it a hobby worth pursuing.

- **Research before you search:** Look into possibly valuable coins on respected sources like the *Numismatists Guaranty Corporation* or the *Professional Coin Grading Service* (Zetlin, 2019). Seek expert advice when you believe you have stumbled across an exceptional find. Numismatic buyers and sellers can be an excellent resource, providing insights and mentoring as you delve deeper into the hobby.
- **Consider the quest for perfection:** For a unique approach, focus on finding uncirculated mint-state coins from recent or current years. Inspect these coins meticulously for the highest quality specimens. Coins rated 67 or 68 in pristine condition can be exceptionally valuable. According to experts, "a 68-graded 2017-D cent," for instance, is valued at around $1,300 (Zetlin, 2019).
- **Build relationships with bank tellers:** Establishing a good rapport with bank tellers can be invaluable. Some banks are willing to order coin rolls upon request. Offering small gestures of appreciation, like donuts or pizza, can go a long way in maintaining their support. If one bank is not cooperative, consider seeking a more coin-roll-hunter-friendly institution.
- **Begin at home:** Before heading to the bank, check your surroundings for old jars of change or coins from relatives. Don't exchange these coins at face value without first examining them for hidden treasures. Coins found in this manner are more likely to be older and unsearched by others, increasing your chances of discovering something valuable.

- **Hunt for anomalies:** Coins with unique characteristics or errors can be exceptionally valuable. Keep an eye out for doubled dies. Also, coins with strangely spaced letters or other irregularities can be noteworthy. For instance, the "1992 Close AM Reverse" penny, characterized by the "A and M in AMERICA" touching, can be worth thousands of dollars (Zetlin, 2019).

- **Explore half dollars:** Depending on current silver prices, about $6 can be the worth of a "pre-1965 half dollar (90% silver)," while a value of approximately $2.50 is held by those "dated between 1965 and 1970 (40% silver)." Sellers can secure significantly higher prices for some venerable and unusual half dollars. For instance, "in April 2019, a 1964 Kennedy Half Dollar was sold for a record-breaking $108,000" (Zetlin, 2019).

- **Search for silver:** Before 1965, "dimes, quarters, half dollars, and dollars" were predominantly crafted from silver, making them inherently more valuable than their face value (Zetlin, 2019). You can quickly identify silver coins, as they lack the clad copper layer found in modern coins. According to experts, "a quick glance at the date, or at the edge of the coin," can reveal if it is silver (Zetlin, 2019).

In coin roll hunting, every roll holds the promise of treasures yet to be discovered by those with a keen eye and the determination to explore.

# 3

# THE INVESTMENT POTENTIAL OF COINS

Throughout history, rare and exotic coins have served as a promising avenue for investment, offering the potential for substantial profits that extend beyond the mere value of the metal in the coin.

According to insights from Finest Known, a newsletter dedicated to rare coins, elite coin values experienced remarkable surges, with prices skyrocketing by more than 1,000% from 1976 to 1980 and a notable 600% increase observed between 1982 and 1989 (Nelson, 2023).

Since the 80s, the rare coin market has undergone substantial changes. Third-party grading services emerged, alleviating investment risks by verifying coin authenticity and establishing standardized grading criteria.

Recently, the Internet Age has revolutionized access to knowledge about coin collecting, rare coins, and coin purchasing, offering a plethora of information and resources to enthusiasts and investors.

## COINS AS TANGIBLE ASSETS

The intriguing realm of rare coin collection presents a captivating and often underestimated opportunity for those aiming to broaden their investment horizons—especially if their primary focus is traditionally on stocks and bonds. Rare coins hold an allure rooted in the potential for sustained financial growth, although it's crucial to recognize that they are not a conduit for rapid, short-term profits. Instead, they beckon with the promise of long-term stability and appreciation.

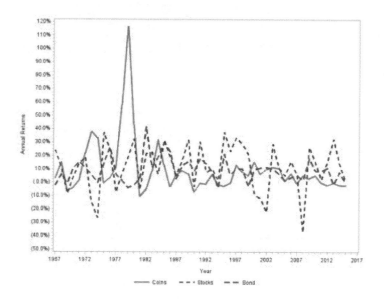

Insights gleaned from research by seasoned market professionals illuminate the historical performance of collectible coins, a journey spanning a remarkable 48-year odyssey from 1967 to 2015. Within this extensive dataset, the narrative unfolds of collectible coins consistently delivering an annual fiscal gain of 9.7%, accompanied by a substantive real return of 5.5%. Over nearly half a century, this steadfast performance underscores the dependable nature of collectible coins as an investment asset (Maslar et al., 2019).

At the heart of sound investment principles lies the art of risk management, and diversification reigns supreme as a linchpin strategy in this pursuit. By embracing the inclusion of precious metals and rare coins within your investment portfolio, you forge a natural bulwark against the erosive forces of inflation. This pivotal attribute distinguishes them from digital assets such as Bitcoin, which often traverse a landscape marked by significant short-term undulations (Anderson, 2022).

Yet, what truly sets precious metals and rare coins apart is their tangible essence. Unlike the undulating dance of stocks and bonds, perpetually influenced by the rhythms of the stock exchange, these assets find solace in the ability to be safely stored and tended to. This autonomy from the traditional financial market provides a compelling advantage, diminishing their exposure to vulnerabilities like cyber threats, frequently besieging their digital counterparts.

Moreover, their innate stability positions them as a beacon for investors seeking to shield their wealth from erratic and volatile market conditions. Even amidst periods of inflation, these assets' value has witnessed a significant ascension. Coins graced with valuable metal content and bearing the mark of extraordinary rarity hold the alluring promise of bequeathing substantial returns over time.

Their enduring stability is a sturdy anchor amidst the tumultuous seas of the stock market and an array of alternative investment avenues. Rare coins, therefore, beckon as a singular opportunity for diversification and the preservation of wealth nestled within the embrace of an investment portfolio.

Rare coins merit thoughtful contemplation for those seeking to enrich the palette of their investment portfolios and fortify their defenses against the perils associated with a myopic fixation on traditional assets such as stocks and bonds. While they may not immediately receive swift profits, their historical performance and palpable essence cast them as an enticing choice for investors charting a course toward long-term financial security and growth. In an ever-evolving investment landscape, the enduring appeal of rare coins remains steadfast, a testament to their resilience and capacity to flourish with time.

## MARKET TRENDS AND PREDICTIONS

The world of numismatics is buzzing with energy and growth. In 2022, it was valued at a whopping $8.7 billion, and here's the exciting part—it is on track for some impressive expansion. Experts anticipate a Compound Annual Growth Rate (CAGR) of 10.4% from 2023 all the way to 2031. That means by 2031, this thriving industry could be worth an astounding $20.9 billion (*Coin Collection*, n.d.). It's an upward trajectory that's hard to ignore.

What keeps this industry pulsating with life is the dedication and passion of collectors and dealers. They are not just chasing dollars; they are captivated by the historical tales and intricate craftsmanship embodied in every coin. These men and women are pivotal in preserving, documenting, and sharing the fascinating stories hidden within these little pieces of history. They are the ones making sure that coin lore stays alive for both enthusiasts and scholars. Their commitment to the past and artistry paints a vivid picture of a lively and ever-evolving coin-collecting world, one that is destined for growth and continued relevance.

A big player in determining a coin's value is its condition. The more a coin has been around, the more it's likely to show signs of wear and tear. Unfortunately, that often translates to a dip in its market value.

But that's not all. The demand for a specific coin can make waves in its market value. When there's a buzz and people are clamoring for a particular coin, you can bet your bottom dollar its price will rise accordingly. It is supply and demand in action. Conversely, when a coin loses its luster and interest dwindles, its market value likely dives. It's like a mesmerizing interplay between a coin's allure and its intrinsic value, and this dynamic is a key element that adds to the intrigue of coin collecting.

The condition of a coin and the ebb and flow of demand are like the rhythm and melody of this unique world. So, whether you're an enthusiast or just curious, remember there's more to coins than meets the eye. It is a world where passion, history, and artistry collide, and it's poised for an exciting journey ahead.

## COIN INVESTMENT STRATEGIES

Short-term and long-term investments follow distinct timelines, each with unique characteristics. Short-term investments involve holding assets for less than a year and, in some cases, for only a few weeks, a strategy commonly adopted by day traders. In contrast, long-term investments necessitate a longer commitment, often spanning a duration of 5 to 10 years or even more (StashTeam, 2023). When we relate these strategies to coins, the long-term plan is always the most lucrative.

For those seeking financial gains from numismatic instruments, strategy emerges in the quest for an undiscovered niche within numismatics (Heller, 2023). It is akin to setting sail on a voyage of exploration. Your journey begins with collecting existing research from books, publications, or online sources. This first step is crucial, as you need to gain insights into pricing dynamics and item availability relative to the number of collectors drawn to that niche. Perform this market research to find coins in niches with a high or (preferably) gradually rising demand that you can buy without breaking the bank. Then, the adventure can commence once you arm yourself with this foundational knowledge.

The next step involves acquiring pieces within this niche while weaving connections with fellow collectors and dealers specializing in this particular category (Heller, 2023). It's like forging bonds with seasoned explorers, sharing insights and discoveries along the way.

As the journey progresses, build your knowledge around this specific numismatic niche, focusing on details that might remain hidden from the broader collector community. Use your information base as the foundation for a series of research articles like chronicles of the expedition. Publish your articles through third-party coin-selling companies or online, promoting your finds in Facebook groups and other platforms. Both of these methods will attract collectors and dealers eager to engage. They may come forth to offer items for sale or to seek further enlightenment about your niche, fostering a vibrant exchange of knowledge and artifacts.

Throughout this numismatic journey, the numismatist often stumbles upon several noteworthy discoveries, like unearthing hidden treasures. These discoveries, in turn, inspire the creation of more research articles, each adding a new chapter to the unfolding narrative. The publication of such research acts as a beacon, illuminating the numismatic niche and drawing an increasing number of collectors into its orbit.

The surge in interest naturally translates into heightened demand for items within this niche (Heller, 2023). Synonymous with a thriving marketplace, the increased demand often results in elevated prices for these numismatic treasures, adding a layer of financial reward to the journey.

Ultimately, when you have achieved your goals in exploring and collecting within this particular numismatic niche, you may choose to part with their collection. This moment symbolizes the culmination of the expedition, a return home with newfound treasures in tow. The financial advantages gained from this endeavor are a monument to the explorer's and researcher's commitment and inventiveness in numismatics.

## ESSENTIAL TIPS TO AVOID GETTING SCAMMED ONLINE

On September 9th, 2021, a stark alert issued by the Federal Bureau of Investigation (FBI) brought a troubling pattern to the forefront—a disquieting surge in the sale of fraudulent coins through various online platforms and social media channels (FBI, 2021).

This worrisome development primarily affects investors and collectors who may unwittingly fall prey to dishonest cyber-criminals selling fake coins as authentic pieces. The FBI has categorized these bogus coins into three distinct groups: "transactional coins (including quarters and dimes), numismatic coins (valuable collectibles), and bullion (precious metals)" COVID-19 (FBI, 2021).

Highlighting the gravity of this issue, in April 2021, officers from the U.S. Customs and Border Protection (CBP) stationed at Chicago's bustling international mail facility intercepted close to 300 shipments from China, each concealing counterfeit coins and currency.

Officials reported in 2020 that the CBP confiscated over "$1.64 million in counterfeit cash and coins at Chicago O'Hare

International Airport" (FBI, 2021). These incidents underscore the magnitude of the problem and the pressing need for increased vigilance in the face of counterfeit coin schemes.

Amidst the challenges of 2021, novice online investors encountered a unique set of hurdles driven by the coin shortage stemming from the COVID-19 pandemic. This scarcity posed a significant dilemma for individuals seeking investment opportunities through online platforms. For these aspiring investors, the digital marketplace represented an alluring avenue, offering convenience, accessibility, competitive pricing, and the promise of doorstep delivery.

In response to these distinctive circumstances, the FBI stepped forward with guidance aimed at safeguarding the interests of these investors. The bureau's counsel is straightforward: exercise caution. The FBI strongly advocates for transactions with established and registered coin dealers known for their legitimacy and trustworthiness.

In cases where dealings extend beyond these reputable confines, the FBI advises an additional layer of protection—having coins independently scrutinized and authenticated by certified organizations. According to the FBI's public service announcement, investors should: "Check online reviews and Better Business Bureau complaints before making a purchase" (FBI, 2021). This proactive measure shields against potential scams and counterfeit coins, bolstering the security and authenticity of investors' endeavors.

## HOW TO AVOID BUYING COUNTERFEIT COINS

### *Research Sellers and Platforms Thoroughly*

- **Check seller reputation:** Look for reviews from other buyers and see if the seller has been reported for selling counterfeit coins on a website like https://www.scamadviser.com/.
- **Use platforms that verify authenticity:** Some coin marketplaces offer authenticity guarantees. This means that if you buy a counterfeit coin from a seller on the platform, the platform will reimburse you for your purchase (*Free online coin cataloging software,* n.d.)

### *Educate Yourself on Counterfeits*

Learn coin characteristics that counterfeiters often overlook. There are certain characteristics of coins that counterfeiters often have difficulty replicating. These include (Bank of Mexico, n.d.):

- **Weight and size:** Counterfeit coins are often made of cheaper metals and may be slightly off-weight or off-size.
- **Edge detail:** Counterfeit coins may have poorly defined edges or casting seams visible to the naked eye.
- **Surface finish:** Counterfeit coins may have a dull or uneven surface finish.

Refer to reliable reference materials/resources for authenticating coins. Many books and websites can help you learn how to authenticate coins. Ensure any resources you use are affiliated with reputable numismatic organizations, such as the American Numismatic Association (ANA) and the Professional Numismatists Guild (PNG).

### Secure Payment Methods and Privacy

- **Use secure payment platforms/payment methods:** When buying coins online, use a secure payment platform such as PayPal or a credit card. These platforms offer buyer protection in case you receive a counterfeit coin.
- **Protect personal information:** When buying coins from a private seller, be careful about sharing your personal information. Only give out your Social Security number or bank account information if you are absolutely sure that the seller is legitimate.

By following these tips, you can help protect yourself from buying counterfeit coins.

## CASE STUDY: THE ERIC P. NEWMAN STORY

Eric P. Newman, a distinguished St. Louis attorney and a dedicated philanthropist, embarked on his remarkable journey into coin collecting at the age of seven. This captivating voyage commenced when his grandfather bestowed upon him a cherished 1859 Indian Head cent.

Over time, Newman's fascination with numismatics deepened, propelling him into the field's echelons of utmost respect and esteem. His collection, lovingly assembled over an astonishing span of 90 years, garnered recognition as one of the most illustrious and invaluable in the entire United States (Healey, 2014).

In 2013, Newman made a profound decision that would mark the culmination of his lifelong passion and leave an enduring legacy. He opted to part with his cherished collection, entrusting it to Heritage Auctions for a series of sales. The proceeds from these sales were dedicated to the Eric P. Newman Numismatic Education Society, a non-profit organization founded by Newman.

These auctions, which unfolded for five years, transcended mere monetary transactions; they transformed into a grand testament to a lifetime devoted to numismatic treasures. The final tally exceeded a staggering $72.9 million, a testament to Newman's life's work's enduring allure and significance (Healey, 2014).

*Actionable Takeaways and Key Strategies*

1. **Start early and exercise patience:** Eric P. Newman's journey into coin collecting began during his youth, highlighting the importance of initiating your collection early. Understand that coin collecting is a pursuit that demands patience and a long-term outlook. Rapid financial gains are not the primary objective; rather, it's about the enduring passion for numismatics.

2. **Invest in education:** Newman's status as a respected numismatic scholar underscores the significance of knowledge in this field. Invest time in educating yourself about coins and their history. Read books, engage in research, and expand your understanding. In coin collecting, knowledge empowers you.

3. **Prioritize quality over quantity:** Newman's collection stood out due to the exceptional quality of its pieces. Many were considered the finest examples available. Instead of amassing numerous coins, focus on acquiring high-quality specimens. Quality often holds more excellent value than quantity in coin collecting.

4. **Collect what you love:** Newman's motivation for collecting coins was driven by his genuine love for them, not merely as investments. Emulate this approach by gathering coins that resonate with your passion and interests. When you collect what you love, the intrinsic value transcends monetary considerations, ensuring you derive joy from your collection regardless of its financial worth.

5. **Consider strategic selling:** If and when you decide to part with your collection, do so thoughtfully. Seek reputable avenues for selling, such as established auction houses. Eric P. Newman's decision to sell his collection through Heritage Auctions exemplifies this. Additionally, consider philanthropic options like donating proceeds to non-profit organizations, as Newman did with the Eric P. Newman Numismatic Education Society.

Remember, your collection could leave a lasting legacy beyond its tangible form.

# 4

## COIN GRADING AND VALUATION

Immerse yourself, for a moment, in the heart of a grading facility. Imagine positioning a coin beneath the scrutiny of a powerful microscope. Armed with a wealth of experience and expertise, the grader casts their discerning gaze upon the coin's surface, leaving no detail unexamined.

Every line, every mark, every seemingly inconsequential feature undergoes rigorous evaluation. The room hums with activity as the grader's intense focus delves into the coin. What was once a simple piece of metal has become a repository of stories etched indelibly onto its surface. Each scratch, tarnish spot, and sign of wear is a chapter in its history.

Yet, within this science of numismatics, a curious paradox unfurls: How is it that something as minuscule as a barely discernible scratch or a faint blemish can wield such an astonishing influence over the value of a coin?

These imperceptible imperfections, often escaping notice by the unassisted eye, possess a remarkable potency. They can tip the delicate balance between a coin's worth resting at mere face value and ascending to the heights of a veritable fortune.

How frequently do we, as individuals, unwittingly overlook the significance of small details? What hidden treasures might we unearth if we invested the time and effort to truly perceive them?

With its unwavering commitment to precision and discernment, numismatics is a testament to the profound value concealed within life's minutiae.

## UNDERSTANDING COIN GRADING

A coin's grade serves as a comprehensive evaluation encompassing two pivotal facets (*Coin grading,* 2018):

- **Refinement:** When considering coin grading, the coin's refinement often takes center stage. Coins with impeccable authenticity and devoid of defects are typically appraised based on their refinement grade. Astonishingly, the market's appetite for a coin graded a single point higher than an identical specimen can oscillate between a few dollars and several hundred thousand dollars.
- **Genuine origin:** In an age where counterfeit coins are growing in sophistication, the authenticity of a coin holds an unprecedented level of importance. The

bustling coin market necessitates unwavering diligence to confirm every coin's legitimacy.

This entire process orbits around an extraordinary mastery honed through years of meticulous scrutiny of minute coin intricacies—artistry aptly christened *coin grading* (*Coin grading,* 2018). This expertise decisively molds a coin's perceived value in collectors' and specialists' discerning eyes.

Coin grading, admittedly, can be a somewhat bewildering endeavor, but it need not remain so. While mastering the art of grading coins remains a formidable task, comprehending the grades can prove invaluable when assessing and acquiring coins.

Numismatics became the talk of the town throughout the 20th century, and both collectors and dealers alike came to a shared realization—not all coins designated as *fine* were created equal. Some were tarnished more than others. These discrepancies, while substantial within the *fine* grade, were further amplified within the *uncirculated* category. To address this, descriptive expressions such as *very fine, extremely fine,* and *gem uncirculated* began to gain prominence and widespread usage (*Coin grading,* 2018).

This quest for precision and accuracy in grading reached its apex in 1949 when Dr. William Sheldon introduced a numerical grading scale, ranging from 1 to 70, to evaluate coins (*Coin grading,* 2018). This pioneering system aimed to provide a more standardized and exacting means of assessing a coin's condition, ultimately contributing to the refinement and sophistication of modern coin grading practices.

In the realm of collectible coins, pondering their value necessitates an unwavering focus on a crucial factor: their condition. In essence, a coin's condition hinges upon the meticulous grading process, and this grade, in turn, profoundly influences its monetary worth. A coin boasting a flawless mint grade commands a significantly higher value than its identical counterpart, marred by even the tiniest imperfection.

The criteria employed to ascertain a coin's grade revolve around a medley of elements, including its allure, coloration, luster, precision of strike, and overall state of preservation. Frequently, coins undergo the scrutiny of impartial third-party grading agencies to determine their grade with the utmost objectivity.

Therefore, when acquiring a coin as a prized collectible, exercise due diligence by selecting a certified specimen and meticulously assessing its grade. This prudent approach ensures that your coin aligns with your discerning standards and retains its rightful place within the world of numismatic treasures.

## GRADING PROCESS AND TECHNIQUES

The grading journey typically unfolds through a series of well-defined stages. Every coin undergoes an initial step, where it is received and logged into a comprehensive database.

Subsequently, these coins transition to the grading chamber, a sacred space where seasoned graders, armed with finely honed expertise, scrutinize them to the minutest particulars. These professionals are adept at uncovering even the most inconspicuous flaws.

The graders assess the wear and tear etched upon each coin and its intrinsic physical attributes. These include the luminous quality of its luster, the captivating palette of its coloration, and the precision of its strike.

Upon reaching the culmination of this meticulous process, the professionals bestow the coins with their final grades. These coins are then carefully placed within individual containers, each preserving its unique distinction and, potentially, its place in the annals of numismatic history.

In the intricate process of coin grading, it becomes paramount to keenly observe and identify the prevailing markers of wear and imperfections. These telltale signs encompass a spectrum of distinctive attributes, each holding the potential to shed light on a coin's condition. Here are some factors that significantly affect a coin's value (Sutevski, 2022):

- **Hairlines:** These are fine scratches on the surface of a coin, usually caused by improper cleaning or wiping. They can reduce a coin's luster and eye appeal and lower its grade. Hairlines are more visible on proof coins than on circulation coins. An example of hairlines is illustrated below:

- **Contact marks:** These are minor nicks, dings, or gouges on a coin, usually caused by other coins or objects hitting or rubbing against it. They can affect the design and detail of a coin and lower its grade. Contact marks are more common on circulation coins than on proof coins. An example of contact marks is illustrated below:

- **Cleaning damage:** This is any damage to the surface or metal of a coin, usually caused by improper or excessive cleaning methods. It can include the following:

  ○ **Abrasion:** The damage caused to a coin's surface when it comes into contact with a rough or abrasive material.
  ○ **Polishing:** The removal of the coin's natural patina or toning through a cleaning process. While it may make a coin appear shiny and new, it often causes damage by altering the coin's original surface and removing a layer of metal.
  ○ **Whizzing:** This is a deceptive cleaning method where a rotating wire brush or abrasive tool artificially creates luster on a coin's surface.
  ○ **Dipping:** This involves submerging a coin in a chem-

ical solution, typically an acidic one, to remove tarnish or surface contaminants.

○ **Plating:** The application of a thin layer of metal, such as gold or silver, onto the surface of a coin. While plating doesn't necessarily cause damage, it can deceive collectors about a coin's actual composition and value if not disclosed.

Cleaning damage can remove a coin's original luster and patina and lower its grade.

Within the vibrant coin-collecting community, third-party grading services emerge as vital pillars. Their role assumes paramount significance, as they serve as impartial and detached evaluators, bestowing each coin an independent, unbiased verdict regarding its authenticity and condition.

This objective assessment provides a twofold advantage. It instills confidence within prospective buyers, assuring them of the coin's genuineness and quality. Simultaneously, it extends a measure of certainty to sellers, who can glean insights into the coin's precise value.

One of the hallmark advantages of entrusting a coin to a third-party grading service is the encapsulation of the coin within a protective holder. Crafted from inert materials, these holders shield the coin from potential harm while cradled within. This protective casing enhances the coin's intrinsic value and augments its security and liquidity, giving collectors and investors peace of mind.

Third-party grading services are guardians of numismatology, ushering in an era of trust and reliability and safeguarding coin treasures (Sutevski, 2022).

## THE ART OF PRESERVING COIN QUALITY

Ensuring the proper preservation of your coin collection is crucial to maintaining its value and integrity. Here are five straightforward steps to follow:

1. **Choose suitable storage supplies:** Select the right storage supplies for your coin collection. A wide array of options are available, including coin holders, folders, albums, and capsules. These may be better to show off your collection to guests. Some coin holders are designed for specific coin sizes and offer airtight protection. These are useful if your main focus is preserving your coins. While others, like cardboard 2x2s, are beginner-friendly options (*Coin collecting supplies*, n.d.).

2. **Exercise caution when cleaning:** Cleaning coins can be risky and potentially lead to surface damage. If you find it necessary to clean your coins, follow the guidelines provided by the United States Mint to minimize the risk of harm. This includes handling coins carefully and wearing gloves, especially when dealing with collectible coins or after cleaning. Furthermore, keeping your coins dry and storing them appropriately is essential to prevent moisture-induced discoloration (Holdefehr, 2023).

3. **Handle coins with care:** When handling your coins, take special precautions to prevent wear and avoid introducing substances that could lead to spots or changes in color. Utilize coin holders to provide essential protection during handling. Always grasp coins between your thumb and index finger while handling them, and consider using a soft pad or towel beneath them to avoid surface abrasions (Holdefehr, 2023).

4. **Implement effective organization and labeling:** Maintain an organized and well-documented record of your coin collection to keep track of your coins and monitor their performance as numismatic investments. You can employ various methods to catalog your collection, such as using a three-ring binder with paper and pen or specialized coin collection software (Bucki, 2021).

5. **Control the storage environment:** Create an ideal storage environment for your coin collection characterized by cool, dry, and dark conditions with low humidity levels. This method safeguards your coins against environmental factors like humidity, acids, and air pollution that could cause damage. Enhance security by investing in a safe to protect high-value coins. Additionally, you can prevent rust and oxidation by placing silica gel packs near your coins to absorb excess moisture, which can hasten tarnishing (Bucki, 2021).

By adhering to these simple yet crucial steps, you can ensure the longevity and value of your cherished coin collection.

## VALUATION FUNDAMENTALS

Multiple factors come into play when determining the value of a coin. These elements collectively contribute to the coin's valuation within the numismatic community:

- **Intrinsic attributes:** A coin's metal content, condition, and bullion worth are key determinants of its value. The purity of the metal, its condition (whether in a pristine or worn state), and the presence of precious metals can significantly influence its worth (*How to work out,* n.d.).
- **Collectability and rarity:** Collectors often seek out coins with unique or limited attributes. Factors like rarity, mintage numbers, and population estimates (how many of that coin are known to exist) play a crucial role in determining a coin's desirability and value (*How to work out,* n.d.).
- **Market dynamics:** Supply and demand in the coin market are paramount. The availability of a particular coin in a specific grade directly impacts its price. The initial mintage of a coin sets the stage for its total possible supply, affecting its market value (MFEATeam, 2023).
- **Survival rate:** Certain coins may have low survival rates due to wars or other historical events, further enhancing their rarity and, subsequently, their value.
- **Minting errors:** Errors during the coin minting process can create rare variations that captivate collectors, making these coins more valuable.

- **Historical significance:** A coin's age, design, and historical context can elevate its worth. Coins from specific eras or regions may carry historical importance that adds to their value (MFEATeam, 2023).
- **Online and offline resources:** To assess a coin's value, you can use various resources. Online platforms like past auction records and the Numismatic Guaranty Corporation (NGC) offer insights into coin values and historical data. Offline coin dealers and numismatists can also provide valuable information about coin history and trends (*How to determine,* n.d.).

By considering these factors and consulting relevant resources, collectors, and investors can better understand and assess the value of their coins.

## PRICE GUIDE AND MARKET PRICING

Coin collectors, whether newcomers or seasoned experts in numismatics, greatly depend on coin price guides and catalogs as essential references. These invaluable resources offer an extensive wealth of information concerning the values of various coins, providing collectors with a comprehensive understanding of the market to facilitate their buying and selling endeavors.

Coin price guides and catalogs provide a comprehensive and detailed overview of coin values, making them akin to encyclo-pedias of coin knowledge. For example, the World Coin Price Guide covers a vast spectrum of world coins from the 1600s to the present day. Collectors can find current values and essential specifications such as weight, composition, engraver details, and prevailing bullion values within its pages. These references serve as indispensable compendiums of coin wisdom, offering a treasure trove of information for collectors of all experience levels.

Delving into recent auction results becomes imperative to acquire the most precise and up-to-date pricing information. Platforms like PCGS Auction Prices are invaluable resources, offering comprehensive historical data on significant coins sold at auctions dating back to 1997. Similarly, NGC World Auction Central provides access to past and upcoming auctions featuring certified world coins, encompassing sales from some of the most prominent numismatic auction houses globally. By examining auction outcomes, collectors gain dynamic insights into current market valuation trends, helping them make informed decisions regarding their collections.

Market fluctuations are part of the game in the ever-evolving realm of coin collecting. Various factors, including shifts in metal prices, changes in collector demand, economic conditions, and more, can influence these fluctuations. For instance, rare coins appreciate over time due to their historical significance and limited availability. Remaining well-informed about these pricing dynamics is crucial for collectors. It will equip you with the knowledge to navigate the market adeptly and make informed choices when acquiring or selling coins.

Coin price guides and catalogs are like trusted companions on a collector's journey, offering guidance through the intricacies of coin values and market trends. Whether you are just starting or are a seasoned collector, these resources are invaluable aids, enhancing your understanding of numismatics and enriching your coin-collecting experience.

## RED BOOK AND BLUE BOOK

The Red Book and Blue Book are esteemed companions for U.S. coin collectors. Within their pages, these books offer indispensable insights into coin identification, grading, and pricing, albeit with distinct characteristics.

- **Red Book:** The Red Book reigns supreme in U.S. coin reference. It comprehensively covers all facets of U.S. coinage, from colonial beginnings to modern issues. Dive deep into its pages, and you'll uncover a treasure trove of information on each coin, including mintage figures, approximate values, historical context, minting locations, grading standards, and guidance on spotting counterfeit coins. Moreover, it presents retail prices based on coin condition, rarity, and market demand.
- **Blue Book:** The Blue Book can be considered the precursor to the Red. It delves into similar U.S. coin types, although with a tad less historical detail and fewer illustrations. For collectors, it offers a section on coin grading and helpful advice on launching a collection. Notably, it provides wholesale price points based on coin condition and rarity (Coreen, 2021).

## *Choosing Your Guide*

The Red Book is an excellent starting point for newcomers to coin collecting. Its comprehensive coverage illuminates U.S. coin history, value assessment, and grading.

Experienced collectors or those contemplating coin sales may find the Blue Book valuable for estimating coin values. However, remember that both books are guideposts; actual coin prices can fluctuate depending on market dynamics (Coreen, 2021).

Ultimately, coin collecting extends beyond mere monetary value. Embrace this hobby as an enriching journey through American numismatics and history.

## CASE STUDY: THE JOURNEY OF A COIN'S VALUE— THE MORGAN DOLLAR

The Morgan Dollar, a silver coin produced by the United States Mint between 1878 and 1904, with a brief revival in 1921, offers a fascinating illustration of the evolution of a coin's worth (*Buy gold & silver,* 2016).

In its early days, the value of the Morgan Dollar was intrinsically linked to the price of silver. With each coin containing roughly 0.7734 ounces of silver, its worth directly mirrored the fluctuations in the global silver market. This straightforward connection between the coin and the precious metal it consisted of was a defining characteristic of its initial valuation.

However, as time progressed, additional factors influenced the coin's value.

Throughout its history, a diverse array of factors has molded the value of the Morgan Dollar. One of the most crucial determinants of a Morgan Dollar's worth revolves around its rarity and the quantity minted in a particular year. Some years and mint marks stand out as exceptionally rare, elevating their desirability and, consequently, their market value.

An illustrative example is the 1895 Morgan Dollar from the Philadelphia Mint, renowned for its exceptionally low mintage, rendering it highly sought-after by collectors. Another pivotal aspect that significantly shapes a Morgan Dollar's value is its condition and overall grade. As discussed, coins in pristine condition, displaying minimal signs of wear and tear, consistently command higher prices within the market.

Market demand exerts its sway on the value of Morgan Dollars, often responding to economic fluctuations and shifts in the demand for silver and silver coins. These dynamic factors can lead to notable volatility in their overall worth.

In the modern landscape of numismatics, Morgan Dollars remain actively traded, with their value continuously influenced by these enduring elements. As of 2023, for instance, a 1921 Morgan Dollar in good condition is valued at approximately $20, while an uncirculated 1895 Morgan Dollar from the Philadelphia Mint can fetch an impressive sum exceeding $40,000 (*Buy gold & silver*, 2016).

This valuation serves as a testament to the interplay of rarity, condition, and market demand, reiterating the multifaceted nature that underpins the evaluation of numismatic treasures over time.

# 5

# COIN HUNTING STRATEGIES AND ADVENTURES

oin hunting, a captivating and modern incarnation of treasure seeking, is very much alive and thriving in today's world. The tales of amateur collectors stumbling upon coins that rewrite history or hold substantial monetary value are not uncommon, from ancient Roman denarii buried in a farmer's field to elusive error coins minted by mistake.

For those who believe treasure hunting belongs to a bygone era, think again. Some people dream of finding buried treasure, but for coin hunters, the thrill is in the hunt itself. A remarkable coin discovery close to my heart occurred when my dear friend Alex, a lifelong numismatist, stumbled upon a 1966 Kennedy Half Dollar in an old barn on a property he had just purchased. He described it as finding a needle in a haystack.

The coin was hidden in a dusty tin box among old tools and junk. He could not believe his eyes when he saw the gleaming silver coin. It's currently worth just under $100, but to Alex, it is priceless. It is a piece of history, a mystery, and a reward for his passion.

Coin hunters never know what they might find. Each coin has a story to tell, a glimpse into the past that can reveal secrets, mysteries, and wonders.

## THE ALLURE OF COIN HUNTING

Coin hunting is not just a hobby or a passion; it is a captivating journey that beckons to those drawn by the allure of uncovering hidden treasures in diverse corners of the world. Imagine it as a modern-day treasure hunt, where enthusiasts like you use metal detectors to seek out coins that time has forgotten, lost, or buried. The possibilities are as endless as the coins themselves.

Metal detectors are your trusty companions on this adventure, but they are not the only tools in your arsenal. Some seasoned coin hunters bring along maps, delve into historical records, or scour online databases to pinpoint promising sites for their quest. It is like being a detective on a mission to unearth history.

It's needless to mention the thrill of the hunt. Coin hunting is like opening a mystery book where every page holds a surprise. You never quite know what you will stumble upon. It could be a coin carrying centuries of weight, like an ancient medieval relic. Alternatively, you may discover coins that mark pivotal historical moments minted during events that shaped nations.

These can be your ticket to an exciting coin trading and appreciation world.

Nevertheless, there's more to coin hunting than just finding valuable artifacts. It's an incredible way to immerse yourself in the great outdoors, all while gaining a deeper understanding of history and culture. You could find yourself in serene parks, along tranquil beaches, through vast fields, or amidst the enchanting depths of forests. Coin hunting lets you soak in nature's beauty as you search for these historical treasures.

The coins you discover are not just relics of the past but portals to history lessons awaiting your exploration. Each coin tells a unique story, offering insights into its era's social, economic, and political conditions. You're not just finding coins; you are becoming a time traveler, delving into the richness of human history.

Another fascinating aspect is that coin hunting often leads to encounters with coins from far-flung corners of the globe. It is like a cultural odyssey, where you come across coins that bear the imprints of different countries and regions. This exposure to diverse cultures and traditions can be as enriching as finding the coins themselves.

So, if you seek an adventure combining the thrill of discovery with the joys of the great outdoors and a deep dive into history and culture, then coin hunting might be the perfect hobby. Who knows what hidden treasures await your keen eye and trusty metal detector?

## SEVEN STEPS TO MAXIMIZE METAL DETECTING SUCCESS

Metal detecting is an incredibly captivating and rewarding hobby that promises thrilling discoveries waiting just beneath the surface. Whether your quest is for ancient coins, historical relics, sparkling jewelry, or even elusive gold nuggets, metal detecting opens up a world of hidden treasures, some of which have remained concealed and untouched for generations.

However, let's not be fooled; metal detection is by no means a Sunday afternoon stroll in the park. It demands a certain level of know-how, skill, and preparation to truly unlock its potential. So, in this section, I will guide you through seven essential steps that will pave your way to becoming a seasoned metal-detecting enthusiast and ensure that you extract the most from this captivating pursuit.

### *How Metal Detectors Work*

One of the first steps to becoming a successful metal detectorist is to learn the basics of how metal detectors work. Metal detectors sense metallic objects by using electromagnetic induction. They consist of a coil of wire that emits a magnetic field when electricity flows through it. This is called the transmitter coil (Woodford, 2023).

When the magnetic field passes over a metal object, it induces an electric current in the object. This current creates another magnetic field around the object, which another coil of wire in the detector, called the receiver coil, picks up. The detector then converts the signal from the receiver coil into an audible tone or a visual indicator that tells you that you have found a metal target (Woodford, 2023).

By understanding how metal detectors work, you can choose the best sensor for your needs and preferences and improve your chances of finding valuable treasures in the ground.

### Choose the Right Metal Detector

Choosing a suitable metal detector is an essential step for coin hunting. You want to find a detector that fits your needs, budget, and the type of coins you are searching for. Here are some factors to consider when choosing a metal detector for coins (Harmer, 2019):

- **Frequency:** The number of times per second a metal detector's coil generates and receives an electromagnetic field is the detector's frequency. Higher frequencies can detect smaller and low-conductivity targets, such as gold nuggets or thin coins, but they are also more affected by ground mineralization and interference. Lower frequencies can penetrate deeper and handle mineralized ground better, but they are less responsive to small or fine targets. For coin hunting, you may choose a detector with a frequency between 5 and 15 kHz, as this range can detect most types of coins effectively.
- **Coil:** The coil is the part of the metal detector that emits and receives the electromagnetic field. Different types

and sizes of coils can affect the performance of your detector. For example, concentric coils have two circles, one inside the other, suitable for pinpointing and discriminating targets. Double-D coils have two overlapping D-shaped coils, effectively covering more ground and dealing with mineralized soil. Monoloop coils have one loop of wire, and they are good for detecting deep and small targets but require a pulse induction detector. For coin hunting, you may choose a coil between 8 and 11 inches in diameter, as this size can provide good depth and sensitivity to coin-sized objects.

- **Discrimination:** A metal detector can reject or accept certain metals based on their conductivity or magnetic properties. This feature can help you filter out unwanted targets, such as iron or trash, and focus on more valuable ones, such as silver or gold. However, discrimination can also eliminate good targets with similar characteristics to the rejected ones, so you must use it wisely and sparingly. For coin hunting, you may choose a detector with a digital target ID or a notch feature that can help you identify the type of coin based on its numerical value or notch segment.

- **Ground balance:** A metal detector can adjust its sensitivity to match the ground conditions, known as ground balance. Highly mineralized ground can cause false signals or mask good targets by creating background noise that confuses the detector. Some detectors have ground balance features that allow you to manually or automatically set the optimal level of sensitivity for the ground you are working on. For coin hunting, I recommend a detector with a ground balance feature, especially if you are detecting in areas with high mineralization, such as saltwater beaches or red clay soils.

## *Choose Suitable Locations*

Choosing suitable locations is one of the most critical factors affecting coin-hunting success. You want to find places with a high probability of containing old and valuable coins and sites that are accessible and legal for metal detecting.

Some of the best places for coin hunting include:

- beaches and lakes
- sidewalk grass strips
- sled hills
- churches (obtain permission)

You should contact local historical societies, museums, libraries, metal detecting clubs, and landowners to get more information and permission to detect on their properties. Always respect their rules and regulations, and never trespass on private or protected lands without consent (MattG, 2023).

Additionally, it's always wise to check the state and local laws regarding metal detecting before you go. Some states require a permit to use detectors on certain state lands, including parks. Some cities also have ordinances prohibiting or restricting

metal detecting on public lands. Always know and follow the
law to avoid any legal trouble.

*Coin Identification*

Once you find a coin with your metal detector, you must identify it correctly to help you determine its value, rarity, and
history. Coin identification involves understanding different
coins' characteristics, such as (*How to identify*, n.d.):

- **Mint mark:** A letter or symbol that indicates where the
  coin was minted. This can help you identify the coin's
  variety and scarcity. As we've discussed, coins may have
  multiple mint marks or none at all.
- **Design:** The images, words, and symbols that appear on
  the coin's obverse and reverse. These can help you
  recognize the coin's theme, style, and meaning. Some
  coins may have artistic designs or political messages.
- **Date:** The year or period when the coin was minted.
  This can help you narrow down the coin's origin and
  series. Some coins may use different date systems than
  the modern ones, such as Roman numerals or lunar
  calendars.
- **Metal:** The type and composition of the coin's metal. A
  coin's metal composition can help determine its quality,
  durability, and authenticity. Some coins may consist of
  precious metals like gold or silver, while others may
  contain base metals like copper or zinc.
- **Denomination:** The face value or unit of currency of
  the coin. This can help you compare the coin's worth

with other coins of the same or different countries. Some coins may have unusual denominations or no denomination at all.

To practice coin identification, you can use sample coins to test your detector's readings and signals for different types of coins. You can also use online tools like coin checkers or price guides to help you identify your coins.

You should also learn to differentiate between coins, trash, and other metal objects that may produce similar signals on your detector. Some common examples of trash items that may fool your detector are pull tabs, bottle caps, nails, foil wrappers, and can slaw (shredded aluminum cans).

To avoid digging up trash items, you can use discrimination features on your detector to filter out unwanted signals based on their metal type or conductivity. However, be careful not to discriminate too much as you may miss some good targets like gold rings or iron relics.

### Master Detecting Techniques

To increase your chances of finding coins with your metal detector, you need to master some basic detecting techniques. These include (*How to use a metal detector*, 2022):

- **Sweeping:** The motion of moving your search coil back and forth over the ground in a controlled manner. You should sweep slowly and steadily at a constant height about 1-2 inches above the ground. To ensure full area coverage, you should overlap your sweeps by about 50% of your coil's width.

- **Pinpointing:** The process of locating a target's exact position and depth after getting a signal from your detector. You can use your detector's built-in pinpoint mode or a handheld pinpointer device to help you pinpoint your target more accurately. You can also use manual methods like cross-sweeping (making an X mark with your coil) or triangulation (making a triangle with your coil) to narrow down your target's location.

- **Digging:** The action of excavating the ground to retrieve your target. You should use appropriate digging tools like trowels, spades, or scoops to carefully extract your target without causing damage to the coin or the environment. You should also dig neat and small holes or plugs that can be easily refilled and restored after you are finished.

### Digging and Retrieval

After pinpointing your target, you must dig and retrieve it safely and responsibly. Here are some tips on how to do that.

Understand how deep different coins might be buried and use the appropriate digging technique. Generally, older coins tend to be deeper than newer coins, as they have been buried longer by natural processes like erosion, sedimentation, and plowing. However, depth can also vary depending on the soil type, moisture, compaction, and interference.

Your detector may indicate the approximate depth of your target based on the signal strength or a depth indicator. You can also estimate the depth using a ruler or a coin probe. Depending on the depth, you may use a trowel for shallow targets or a spade or shovel for deeper targets.

Use digging tools like trowels or pinpointers to carefully extract coins without causing damage to the coin or environment (Harmer, 2023). You should avoid using metal tools that may scratch or dent your coins and instead use gentler plastic or wooden instruments on the metal surface. You should also avoid magnets that may demagnetize your coins or affect their value. Always be mindful of the environment and avoid digging in sensitive areas like archaeological sites, historical landmarks, or wildlife habitats.

Clean your coins properly after retrieving them. You should remove dirt or debris from your coins using a soft brush, cloth, or water. You should avoid using harsh chemicals, abrasives, or metal polishers that may damage your coins or remove their patina. You should also avoid cleaning coins you believe are rare, valuable, or have historical significance, as cleaning may reduce their value or authenticity. In this case, consult an expert before taking any action.

### Document and Learn From Finds

After finding and retrieving your coins, you should document and learn from your finds. This process will help you improve your coin-hunting skills, expand your knowledge, and enjoy your hobby more.

Here are some ways to document and learn from your finds:

- **Record your finds in a logbook or a spreadsheet:** You should jot down the date, location, type, condition, and value of each coin you find. You should also take photos of your coins and attach them to your records to help you keep track of your progress, organize your collection, and share your finds with others.
- **Research each coin you find using online resources or books:** You should learn about the history, culture, and significance of each coin you find. You should also compare your coins with other examples and identify any errors, varieties, or rarities that may increase their value or interest.
- **Return to areas where you have previously found coins:** Caches of coins often group together. Therefore, if you find one, there is a good chance of more nearby.

## TELLING TALES THROUGH COINS: WHAT WE LEARN FROM DISCOVERIES

Have you ever wondered what stories lie behind the coins in your pocket or collection?

One of the first steps in analyzing a coin is to identify its type, which is the central design on the reverse, usually surrounded by a legend. The type can indicate the coin's period, region, ruler, mint, and denomination and the political, economic, religious, and cultural messages the issuer wanted to convey.

Celtic coins are the primary source of information about the Celtic tribes in Britain and Gaul, as they left no written records (Holt, 2021). Their coins show a variety of designs, influenced by Greek, Roman, and native styles, and often bear the names of the tribal leaders or the mints. Their coins also reflect their resistance to Roman expansion, as they imitated and adapted Roman coins to suit their own needs and tastes.

One of the most recent and remarkable numismatic discoveries is the unique Caratacus gold stater, found near Newbury, Berkshire, in 2019, discovered by a metal detectorist (Jewers, 2020). Many consider this coin the most important single Iron Age coin ever found in Britain, as it confirms the identity and lineage of Caratacus, the first British freedom fighter who resisted the Roman invasion. The coin is dated to around AD 40-41, before his capture, and was struck at Calleva (Silchester, Hampshire), the capital of his tribe, the Atrebates (Holt, 2021).

The coin bears the name CARA[TAC] on one side and COMF on the other, which stands for Commius Filius (son of Commius), indicating that Caratacus was the son of Commius, another British king who allied with Julius Caesar in his invasion of Britain in 55-54 BC.

The coin also shows a stylized horse on one side and a wreath on the other, both symbols of Celtic culture and identity. This coin is unique (only one known example) and very valuable for its historical significance, as it directly links to one of the most famous figures in British history (Holt, 2021).

When you look at a coin, you might wonder where it came from and where it has been. You can try to trace its journey and lifecycle, which is the path that the coin followed from the moment it was made to the moment it fell into your possession. This visualization can help you understand how the coin was made, traded, and lost over time. You can also learn about the people and places the coin encountered along the way and how they influenced its shape, value, and meaning.

Another thing you can do with a coin is to evaluate its importance and impact on history. You can see how the coin can add to or change what we know about the past. Sometimes, a coin can provide new or extra information that we don't have from other sources, especially for the times or places that have few or no written or archaeological records.

Other times, a coin can challenge or support what we already think or believe about the past, especially for the times or places with different or conflicting interpretations. Sometimes, a coin can raise or answer new questions we have never thought to ask about the past, especially regarding times or places with interesting or mysterious aspects.

By doing this, you can appreciate how the coin can make history richer and more meaningful for us.

## CASE STUDY: A COIN HUNTER'S TRIUMPH

Step into the shoes of a passionate coin hunter and explore the journey of an individual who turned a love of outdoor exploration into a rich collection of numismatic treasures.

Imagine finding a rare and valuable gold coin that dates back to the 14th century and tells a story of a failed attempt to introduce gold currency in England. That is what happened to Andy Carter, a retired scientist and metal detectorist who made a remarkable discovery in a field in Norfolk, England (Young, 2022).

Andy Carter is a 65-year-old metal detecting enthusiast who lives in Suffolk, England. He has been interested in history and archaeology since childhood and enjoys spending his free time searching for ancient coins and artifacts with his metal detector. He has found hundreds of coins over the years, ranging from Roman to Medieval to Modern periods.

He also found some rare and valuable coins, such as a gold solidus of Emperor Constantine, a silver penny of King Alfred the Great, and a bronze sestertius of Emperor Hadrian. He keeps a detailed record of his findings and often researches each coin's history and significance. He also shares his discoveries with other coin enthusiasts on online forums and social media platforms.

One of his most remarkable finds happened in 2019 when he stumbled upon a hoard of 99 silver coins dating back to the 11th century. He was scanning a field near his home when he got a strong signal from his metal detector. He dug about ten inches into the mud and was amazed to see a cluster of silver coins shining in the soil. He carefully extracted the coins and realized that they were Anglo-Saxon pennies from the reigns of King Ethelred II and King Canute. He contacted the local authorities and reported his find as required by the law.

Experts examined the coins and stated they were treasures under the Treasure Act of 1996. The coins were valued at

£50,000 and offered to a museum for purchase. Andy received a reward of £25,000, which he split with the landowner. He also received a certificate of recognition from the British Museum, and he was invited to see his coins on display (Young, 2022).

He was thrilled to have significantly contributed to his country's numismatic and historical knowledge. Andy is a shining example of a passionate coin hunter who turned his love of outdoor exploration into a rich collection of numismatic treasures.

# THE KEY TO THE TREASURE TROVE

*"Coin collecting is a hobby for boys, an investment for fathers, and a windfall for grandfathers."*

— D.WAYNE JOHNSON

By this stage in the book, you're probably realizing that your collection carries far more depth and intrigue than you'd imagined. Such is the case for many coin collectors: What begins as a hobby kickstarted by one interesting coin grows gradually, and suddenly you're filled with a burning desire to learn more.

From there, your interest only grows, and you start to realize that you have investment opportunities you have yet to consider at your fingertips. A whole world opens up, and you discover you want all the other beginners out there to understand the treasures they're working with – because that's the key to a thriving community rich with opportunities.

I wrote this book to help newcomers to the world of numismatics expand their knowledge and expertise, giving them the key to exploring their passion and discovering everything it has to offer… and now your own horizons are expanding, I'd like to ask you to take a moment to help me spread the word.

This will have a profound impact on beginners who are searching for this information, yet it will take you no more than a few minutes. All you have to do is leave a short review.

**By leaving a review of this book on Amazon, you'll help other beginner coin collectors discover exactly what treasures they're sitting on and help them grow their passion.**

Just as you were, there are coin collectors out there searching for this information, and your review will help them to find it easily.

Thank you so much for your support. There's so much to discover with coin collecting, and when we share information, we open the world up to all the like-minded folk who are interested.

# 6

# THE REALM OF CONNECTING AND NEGOTIATING

O ne of the most enchanting aspects of being part of a coin collector community is the opportunity to forge genuine relationships and share your expertise. Within these communities, you'll encounter kindred spirits who share your fervor for coins. It's not merely about the coins themselves but the tales they narrate.

Coin collecting is more than a mere pastime; it's a captivating journey, and becoming a part of a coin collector community can significantly enhance your numismatic experience. These communities offer many advantages, catering to enthusiasts at all levels, whether you're just starting or a seasoned expert.

## THE BENEFITS OF JOINING COIN COLLECTOR COMMUNITIES

Coin collecting allows you to tap into fellow collectors' collective knowledge and wisdom. Whether you seek advice on identifying and valuing coins or simply yearn to share the thrill of your latest discovery, you are amidst peers who grasp the exhilaration of the quest.

Beyond the digital realm, coin collector communities breathe life into the hobby through tangible experiences like coin shows, fairs, and conventions. These gatherings provide a unique opportunity to submerge yourself in the world of coin collecting. At these conventions, you can walk amid tables laden with coins, engage in conversations with collectors from diverse corners of the globe, and participate in enlightening seminars that deepen your comprehension of the craft. Coin shows offer the chance to buy, sell, and trade coins, all while cultivating connections that transcend geographic boundaries.

In today's interconnected world, online forums and social media groups function as the digital town squares of coin collector communities. These digital platforms serve as treasure troves of knowledge and camaraderie. Here, you can pose queries, solicit advice, and remain informed about the ever-evolving landscape of coin collecting. Share images of your cherished coins, extend invitations for insights from seasoned collectors, and nurture your expertise.

Coin collector communities cater to collectors across the spectrum, ensuring that everyone finds the niche where they belong. For new collectors, local coin clubs provide guidance and companionship. Here, they can acquaint themselves with various coin types, receive counsel on commencing their collections, and absorb the wisdom imparted by seasoned mentors.

Seasoned collectors can explore national coin-collecting organizations, which furnish subscriptions to coin-collecting magazines, exclusive privileges at coin shows, and a treasury of educational resources to deepen their erudition. Start by researching the national coin-collecting organizations that align with your interests.

Some well-known organizations include the American Numismatic Association (ANA) and the Numismatic Literary Guild (NLG). Explore their websites to understand their missions, membership benefits, and fees. As a beginner, joining an organization like the ANA may be wise because they usually offer access to research libraries, online forums, and exclusive publications. These resources can assist you in expanding your collection and understanding the coin market.

For those captivated by the world of rare coins, specialized online forums dedicated to rare coin collecting beckon. These forums are sanctuaries where enthusiasts can refine their discernment of counterfeit coins, stay attuned to market dynamics, and connect with connoisseurs who share their fascination with exceptional numismatic treasures. Websites like the ANA often have active forums. You can sign up for membership on these sites and participate in their coin discussion sections.

Irrespective of your position on the spectrum of coin collecting, a coin collector community is awaiting your participation. These communities are not merely about elevating your collecting endeavor; they are about embarking on a shared journey through the realm of numismatics. So, why hesitate? The gates to discovery and fellowship stand wide open, extending an invitation to join the ranks of passionate coin aficionados.

## FINDING MENTORSHIP AND LEARNING OPPORTUNITIES IN COIN-COLLECTING COMMUNITIES

An array of opportunities awaits within the coin-collecting communities, offering members the chance to embrace learning and intellectual growth through formal channels or in a personal exchange of shared knowledge.

Among the most cherished facets of coin-collecting communities is the chance to glean wisdom from seasoned collectors. These individuals, who have traversed the meandering paths of numismatics, often play the role of mentors. Many coin collector communities boast mentorship programs to pair new enthusiasts with experienced guides. These mentors offer valuable guidance, imparting knowledge about various coin types, techniques for identifying and valuing coins, and strategies for nurturing a burgeoning collection.

Coin-collecting communities extend their educational embrace through both structured and spontaneous means. Formal education may manifest as classes, workshops, and seminars.

These sessions delve into intricate topics like coin identification, coin grading, and the art of coin investing. Informal learning opportunities are just as enriching, often comprising expert talks, engaging field trips to coin museums, and the camaraderie of coin-collecting forums.

Coin collector communities serve as fertile grounds for personal growth and the exchange of wisdom. Within these communities, individuals find a platform to share their coin-related expertise and passion with like-minded peers. By participating in coin collector activities and events, you learn from others and contribute to the collective growth of the coin-collecting community.

## CONDUCTING RESPECTFUL TRANSACTIONS

The relationship between coin collectors and dealers has always been a delicate balance, driven by the expectations of consumers and the profit motives of dealers. This divide between trust and profit maximization often gives rise to misunderstandings and conflicts within the coin-collecting market.

Consumers naturally expect honesty and fairness when dealing with coin dealers. They entrust their cherished collections to these experts, hoping to receive equitable appraisals and prices. However, like any business, dealers aim to maximize their profits, which can sometimes conflict with these expectations. This misalignment of objectives can create a trust deficit that complicates negotiations between collectors and dealers.

As an observer of the coin-collecting market, it's evident that this discord is rooted in the differing perspectives of consumers and dealers. While consumers emphasize fairness and honesty, dealers prioritize profitability. Bridging this gap and fostering trust is essential for a smoother, more satisfying coin-collecting experience.

Understanding the inner workings of the coin market to enhance your negotiation skills when dealing with coin dealers is crucial. Knowledge is your strongest asset in these transactions. Conduct research and educate yourself about the value of your coins. Doing so gives you a realistic assessment of what your collection is worth, empowering you during negotiations.

Here are some tactics to keep in mind when negotiating with coin dealers (Headley, 2022):

- **Do your research:** Before engaging with a dealer, invest time in researching the coins you own. Familiarize yourself with their historical significance, rarity, and current market value. Armed with this knowledge, you can confidently negotiate a fair price.
- **Be prepared to walk away:** If the dealer's offer falls short of your expectations, don't be afraid to walk away. While it might be tempting to settle, holding firm can sometimes lead to a better deal elsewhere. Remember, you have the right to seek offers from multiple dealers.
- **Maintain respectful communication:** Even if negotiations become challenging, always maintain a respectful and professional demeanor. Building a positive rapport with dealers can lead to better

outcomes in the long run. Respectful communication can also help defuse any potential conflicts.

Following these guidelines increases your chances of securing a fair price when buying or selling coins. Ultimately, bridging the trust gap between consumers and dealers is a collective effort, and it begins with informed and empowered collectors who navigate the market with confidence and knowledge.

## ENGAGING IN NUMISMATIC DISCUSSIONS

A few fundamental principles can pave the way for constructive and respectful interactions when engaging in numismatic discussions with other collectors. These principles foster a sense of community and enrich the collective knowledge of coin enthusiasts.

Firstly, participation in informed and respectful debates is paramount. Take the time to do your research before entering a discussion. Being well-prepared adds credibility to your contributions and demonstrates respect for the topic and your fellow participants. Equally crucial is maintaining a respectful demeanor toward the opinions of others, even when disagreements arise. Avoid personal attacks and inflammatory language, as these can hinder productive discourse.

Sharing your knowledge in a manner that doesn't undermine others is another vital aspect of numismatic discussions. When imparting your insights, be mindful of the other person's experience and expertise. Avoid using overly technical jargon that might alienate those less familiar with numismatics. If specialized language is necessary, explain it clearly and concisely, promoting mutual understanding.

Fostering a welcoming and inclusive numismatic community should be at the forefront of every discussion. Numismatics is a hobby for everyone, irrespective of age, gender, race, ethnicity, or experience level. Be conscious of your language and behavior, avoiding assumptions or generalizations about others. Instead, focus on the shared passion for numismatics that unites participants.

In addition to these core principles, consider the following tips for engaging in numismatic discussions:

- **Listen actively:** Pay close attention to what others have to say. Take the time to understand their arguments and perspectives. Active listening promotes a more empathetic and productive conversation.
- **Embrace new ideas:** Numismatics is a complex and ever-evolving field. Be open to new ideas and fresh perspectives. There's always more to learn, and diverse viewpoints can broaden your horizons.
- **Admit mistakes gracefully:** No one is infallible, and mistakes happen. If you're corrected during a discussion, be gracious and acknowledge the correction. Humility fosters a positive and constructive atmosphere.
- **Enjoy the experience:** Numismatics is a captivating and rewarding hobby. Relish the opportunity to share your knowledge and passion with fellow enthusiasts.

The joy of learning and connecting is at the heart of these discussions.

Adhering to these principles and tips can significantly contribute to developing a welcoming and inclusive numismatic community. Together, we can ensure that numismatic discussions remain spaces where everyone feels comfortable participating in informed and respectful conversations.

## COIN COLLECTING FOR GENERATIONS

Coin collecting is a timeless tradition that weaves the threads of generations, forming a bridge that spans the past, the present, and the future. In this section, we delve into the profound significance of imparting the passion for coins from one generation to the next, crafting a legacy characterized by appreciation, continuous learning, and shared experiences.

Coins, often overlooked as mere currency, possess a unique power. They can encapsulate history, art, and culture within their tangible forms. They're more than collectibles; they're invaluable tools for preserving and celebrating your family's heritage, weaving together the threads of generations.

When holding a coin, you're holding a piece of history. Coins carry the imprints of monarchs, the symbols of nations, and the events that shaped societies. When you explore coin collections, you're unraveling the historical tapestry of your ancestors. You're connecting with the past, appreciating the struggles, triumphs, and changes that have woven your family's story.

But it doesn't stop there. Coins are more than historical records; they're miniature canvases where artistry thrives. From intricate engravings to striking designs, coins showcase the artistic achievements of their times. By exploring the artistry of coins, you gain an appreciation for the aesthetics that shaped your family's cultural heritage. You're connecting with the creativity and craftsmanship of the past, fostering a deeper understanding of the artistic traditions passed down through the generations.

Coins also reflect culture, values, and traditions. They bear symbols, inscriptions, and motifs deeply rooted in the cultural fabric of a society. When you study these elements, you gain insights into the values and beliefs that have shaped your family's culture. Coins are tangible reminders of cultural heritage, helping you connect with your roots and celebrate the rich tapestry of traditions that define your family.

To truly make this connection with your heritage through coins, you should listen to the stories and memories shared by older family members. Hearing about the coins they found or inherited provides a personal and emotional connection to the past. These stories become bridges that link the generations, allowing the wisdom and experiences of older family members to be passed down and cherished.

I will never forget the feeling I got when I sat down with my grandfather, hearing about how he and my great-grandfather collected coins during particular historical events or how my great-grandparents received special coins as gifts. These stories preserve family heritage and instill a sense of pride and identity in you. They become a part of a living legacy that transcends time, connecting your family's history, art, and culture in a tangible and meaningful way.

Consider incorporating coins into your family discussions and traditions. It's a journey that allows you to celebrate your roots, connect with your ancestors, and pass down the richness of your family's history, art, and culture to future generations.

## COIN TREASURE HUNT ACTIVITY

Coin collecting is more than a hobby; it's an opportunity to bond with your family and inspire a new generation of collectors. Beyond coins, I will show you how your passion can create lasting family memories and keep the tradition alive for generations. Your love for coins can ignite curiosity and connection within your family. The following is a practical and easy-to-follow activity that you and your family will enjoy.

- **Materials:** Gather a variety of coins, including old and unique ones.
- **Hide the coins:** Bury the coins at various depths in a designated area. Keep a list of their locations.
- **Rules:** Explain the rules and provide historical context for the coins, sharing brief stories or facts about their origin or era.
- **Start the hunt:** Release participants to find the buried coins. They can use metal detectors if available or rely on their intuition and sharp eyes.

- **Educational moments:** As participants find coins, take a moment to discuss each coin's history, country of origin, and any unique features.
- **Prizes:** Consider offering small awards for achievements like finding the most, locating the oldest, or identifying specific coins correctly.
- **Family bonding:** Encourage family members to work together, especially if participants are of different ages. It's an excellent opportunity for the older generation to share their knowledge and enthusiasm with the younger ones.
- **Wrap-up:** Gather everyone to share their experiences and discoveries after the treasure hunt. Create a makeshift coin exhibit where participants can display their finds and discuss them with the rest of the family.

This *Coin Treasure Hunt* combines the excitement of a treasure hunt with educational moments, fostering an interest in coin collecting and history while strengthening family bonds.

# 7

# USING WHAT WE'VE LEARNED— STARTING AND GROWING YOUR COLLECTION

You have made an excellent decision. You are on the path to creating a unique collection and believe me, it will be a fantastic adventure.

Building a first-rate collection isn't just a destination; it is a journey bursting with excitement and endless possibilities. It is going to take some time, dedication, and a whole lot of curiosity, but it is going to be worth it!

As you dive headfirst into the world of collecting, get ready to be amazed. With every new coin you find, you'll expand your knowledge and shape a collection that will be a colorful expression of your personality and interests. I mean it—the happiness and fulfillment you will experience are beyond words.

So, with the knowledge and insights you have unearthed, you are now superbly prepared to embark on this exhilarating collecting expedition. It is a path filled with astonishing discoveries, captivating stories, and the sheer thrill of preserving pieces of history for generations to come.

Once you have defined your budget and chosen your focus, it's time to roll up your sleeves and delve deep into numismatics with your thirst for knowledge. In this chapter, we'll explore the importance of education and research in coin collecting. You will discover how to equip yourself with the insights and skills necessary to become a savvy collector.

Remember, the more you know about the coins you collect, the more informed and rewarding your collecting experience will be. Get ready to collect your way into an exciting new world!

## SET CLEAR GOALS AND FOCUS

Coin collecting is a rewarding hobby that can bring you joy and satisfaction. It allows you to explore history, art, culture, and much more through tangible artifacts. However, it's essential to remember that this hobby can become as diverse as the coins themselves, ranging from affordable to truly extravagant. Before you start, you must set clear goals and focus on what you want to achieve.

- **Define your budget:** Coin collecting, like any hobby or investment, can be as financially flexible as you make it. Setting a realistic budget is not just about limiting your spending; it's a strategic move that empowers you to make informed decisions, avoid impulse buying, and plan your purchases wisely. Your budget acts as your compass in the vast landscape of coin collecting. It provides clear boundaries, allowing you to navigate the market with confidence.

- **Choose a focus:** Coin collecting is a vast field, so you need to narrow down your interests. What kind of coins do you want to collect? Ancient coins, coins from a specific country, commemorative coins, or coins from a particular era? Choosing a focus will help you learn more about your coins and find the ones that suit your taste. You can always expand your collection later, but it's better to start with a clear theme.

## RESEARCH AND LEARN

If your passion for coin collecting burns brightly, your thirst for knowledge in this captivating hobby should be insatiable. In your pursuit of coin-collecting excellence, knowledge is your most precious asset.

- **Educate yourself:** The boundless realm of coin collecting awaits you on the internet. Take advantage of online resources and coin-collecting forums to learn. Dive into comprehensive online guides that cover every facet of coin collecting, from identifying coins to understanding their grading systems and market values. Explore a wealth of written articles, engaging videos, and enlightening podcasts, all dedicated to the world of numismatics. These resources offer invaluable insights into the stories behind the coins you collect.
- **Attend local coin shows:** While the digital realm provides a wealth of information, there's unparalleled

magic in holding coins in your hand and engaging with fellow collectors face-to-face. Rows upon rows of tables at coin shows contain treasures waiting to be discovered. Whether you're a seasoned collector or just starting, coin shows offer a wide range of coins at various price points. At coin shows, seasoned professionals can appraise or grade your coins.

## JOIN COIN COLLECTING COMMUNITIES

If you love collecting coins, join some coin-collecting communities. There are many benefits of being part of a community of like-minded enthusiasts who share your passion and hobby.

- **Online forums:** One of the easiest and most convenient ways to connect with other coin collectors is through online forums and communities. You can browse different topics, ask questions, share insights, and learn from the experts. You can also find out about the latest news, trends, and deals on coins. Online forums are a great way to expand your knowledge and network with collectors worldwide.
- **Local clubs:** Another way to join coin-collecting communities is to look for local clubs in your area. Local clubs are a great way to meet fellow collectors in person, exchange coins, and get tips and feedback. You can also participate in club activities like meetings, discussions, and events. Local clubs often offer opportunities to buy, sell, or trade coins at reasonable prices. You can also enjoy the camaraderie and

friendship of other coin collectors who share your interest.

By joining these communities, you'll enhance your coin-collecting skills and discover cost-effective ways to build your collection.

## START WITH AFFORDABLE COINS

If you want to start a coin collection, here are some tips to help you find beautiful, engaging, and affordable coins. Beginning with affordable and accessible coins allows you to develop your passion for collecting without straining your finances. Over time, you can gradually expand your collection to include rarer and more valuable pieces.

- **Look for common coins with style:** You don't have to spend a fortune to get attractive and unique coins. Many common coins have great designs and features that make them stand out. You can start your collection with these coins and build a solid base for your hobby.
- **Discover coins in circulation:** You can also find coins still being used as money. These coins can be fun to hunt for and collect. You can get them from stores, other coin collectors, or banks by utilizing the coin-roll hunting strategies we've discussed. You might be surprised by the variety and history of the coins you can find in circulation.

As time unfolds, you can gradually set your sights on rarer and more valuable pieces. Every coin you acquire becomes a piece of history, a testament to your dedication, and a source of joy that will accompany you throughout your collecting career.

## SEARCH FOR DEALS

Are you looking for some deals on coins? Finding great deals can be an exciting part of your collecting journey. Whether you are a beginner or an expert collector, you can find some great bargains with these tips:

- **Explore online marketplaces:** You can discover a treasure trove of coins on online auction sites, coin marketplaces, and social media groups. You can snag some rare or valuable coins at low prices if you bid on auctions that end at odd hours or days.
- **Visit coin shops:** Nothing beats browsing a local coin shop and finding something that catches your eye. Coin shops have a wide range of coins for every budget and taste, and you can often find some hidden gems in their "bargain bins" or discount sections.
- **Metal detecting:** If you love the adventure of hunting for coins in the wild, why not try metal detecting? You never know what you might unearth with your detector, and the best part is that it's free! You can add unique and historical coins to your collection without spending a dime.

Exploring these avenues can help you build your collection without straining your finances and make coin collecting an even more rewarding hobby.

## FOCUS ON QUALITY, NOT RARITY

When building your coin collection, remember that quality often surpasses rarity. Here are some tips to help you emphasize quality over scarcity:

- **Prioritize condition:** Don't settle for worn-out or damaged coins, even if they are rare. Look for coins that are in excellent shape, with precise details and minimal flaws. Well-preserved coins tend to be more valuable and offer greater enjoyment in your collection. The intricate details and vibrant appearances of coins in good condition can be truly captivating.
- **Grading knowledge:** Learn how to grade coins using the official standards of the industry. Understanding how to assess a coin's condition accurately is essential. You don't have to become a professional grader, but understanding the basics and gaining an idea of a coin's grade before a purchase is a critical skill for a collector.

With an emphasis placed on quality, you can assemble a collection that holds its value and provides a more visually appealing and satisfying collecting experience.

## PRESERVE YOUR COLLECTION

If you love collecting coins, you know how important it is to keep them in good condition. Coins can lose their value and beauty if they are exposed to dirt, moisture, fingerprints, scratches, or chemicals.

- **Use coin holders:** To preserve your collection, you should use coin holders made of inert materials, such as plastic or cardboard. Avoid holders that contain PVC, which can damage your coins over time.
- **The five coin-preserving steps** (Bucki, 2021):

  - Store your coins in a cool, dry, and dark place.
  - Handle your coins carefully with gloves or tongs.
  - Inspect your coins regularly for signs of damage or deterioration.
  - Clean your coins only if absolutely necessary and with proper methods.
  - Protect your coins from theft or loss by keeping an inventory and insurance.

For passionate coin collectors, the significance of preserving the condition of their cherished coins cannot be overstated. Beyond being mere objects of fascination, coins carry intrinsic value and aesthetic beauty. Yet, they are also delicate artifacts that can lose their luster and worth when subjected to various forms of deterioration.

## GRADUALLY UPGRADE

One of the joys of coin collecting is to see your collection improve over time. As you delve deeper into the world of coin collecting, you'll discover that it's not just about amassing a quantity of coins but also about strategically enhancing the quality and value of your collection. You can do this by following these simple steps:

- **Buy smarter:** Don't just buy any coin that catches your eye. With growing experience and knowledge, your ability to discern undervalued coins with future appreciation potential will improve. Do some research and learn how to spot coins that are underpriced or have a solid potential to increase in value over time. You can use online resources, books, magazines, or experts to help you with this.
- **Trade and sell:** You don't have to keep every coin you buy. Sometimes, you may find that you have duplicates or coins that no longer match your collecting goals. Instead of letting them gather dust, consider trading or selling these coins. You can trade or sell them to other collectors or dealers and use the money to buy better coins that enhance your collection.

By adopting a thoughtful and strategic approach to upgrading your coin collection, you can enhance its overall quality and potentially increase its long-term value and personal satisfaction.

## RESEARCH AND SHARE

As a coin collector, you have the opportunity to explore and enjoy a fascinating world of stories, history, and connections. Every coin you collect has a special meaning and significance, no matter how rare or common. You can enrich your hobby by following these two simple steps:

- **Keep learning and discovering:** Coin collecting never gets boring because there is always something new to learn. Every coin has a story to tell, a history to reveal, and a context to understand. The more you research and satisfy your curiosity, the more you'll appreciate the coins you have and the ones you want to have. Your knowledge and experience will also enhance the value of your collection, both for yourself and others.
- **Network with other collectors:** Coin collecting is not a solitary hobby; it's a social one. You can share your passion and excitement with other collectors, whether they are your friends, family, or members of the wider numismatic community. You can exchange stories and tips, listen to others' perspectives, and join discussions or local coin clubs. These interactions will help you learn more and inspire you to keep pursuing your hobby.

Coin collecting is not just about collecting pieces of metal; it's about assembling pieces of history, culture, and art. By embracing the educational and social aspects of this hobby,

COIN COLLECTING 101 | 111

you'll make your journey as a coin collector more fulfilling and rewarding.

As we conclude this chapter, it's essential to recognize that setting clear goals and maintaining focus are the compass points guiding your adventure. In coin collecting, the journey is as valuable as the coins themselves.

With this chapter's tips and guiding principles, you are equipped to navigate the captivating realm of coin collecting—where every piece becomes a chapter in the story of your passion. May your journey be as enriching as the coins themselves, and may the connections you forge and stories you encounter along the way add immeasurable value to your collection.

# 8

# UNVEILING NUMISMATIC MYSTERIES—RARE AND UNUSUAL COINS

C oins have been around for thousands of years, and tales of lost treasures come with them. We've already covered that certain coins can hold a value far greater than the metal they consist of, but did you know that some even carry concealed messages or symbols, revealing intriguing origins? And then there are the exceedingly rare ones, so scarce that only a fortunate few have ever laid eyes on them.

These captivating facts are just a glimpse into the mesmerizing realm of rare and unusual coins. Whether you are a collector, a history enthusiast, or simply a curious soul, you are in for a journey filled with secrets and astonishments. Prepare to be amazed by the discoveries that await in this fascinating hobby!

## LEGENDS OF LOST COINS

Some of the most captivating tales in the world of coin collecting involve the discovery of lost treasures. Let us dive into a few remarkable stories that reveal the enchantment of unearthing these numismatic wonders.

In 2009, the world was introduced to the Staffordshire Hoard, a collection of Anglo-Saxon gold and silver artifacts. This hoard is the largest ever found in Britain, boasting a staggering value of over £3.2 million. The credit for this astounding discovery goes to Terry Herbert, a dedicated metal detectorist who stumbled upon this treasure trove while scanning a field in Staffordshire (Rodger, 2019).

Fast forward to 2023, and we encounter the Great Kentucky Hoard—a collection of over 700 gold coins from the Civil War era. This remarkable find marks the largest hoard of its kind ever unearthed in the United States. The hoard's anonymous discoverer was metal detecting on his farm in the picturesque Kentucky countryside (Yang, 2023).

Nevertheless, it is not just the grand hoards that capture our imaginations. There are countless stories of people stumbling upon lost coins, each with its unique history. Take, for instance, a fortunate gentleman in England who, in 2022, happened upon a rare gold coin dating back to the time of Edward III while taking a stroll in a field. The coin, now valued at over £10,000, is a testament to the allure of these hidden treasures (Sherwood, 2022).

Discovering a lost coin is not just about the financial windfall; it is a link to the past—a glimpse into the lives of those who came before us. It's the thrill of unearthing a piece of history and the satisfaction of knowing you have uncovered something that lay dormant for centuries.

Stories like these continue to inspire and excite coin enthusiasts worldwide. They remind us that secrets waiting to be revealed fill the world of numismatics and that anyone can become a part of these legends of lost and found coins with a bit of luck, patience, and a keen eye. So, keep your senses sharp and your detectors ready—you never know what treasures might be hiding just beneath the surface.

## UNRAVELING THE ENIGMA OF ERROR COINS

In the world of coin collecting, there exists a fascinating category that never fails to pique the curiosity of numismatists: Error coins. These enigmatic specimens bear unique imperfections resulting from various anomalies in the coin production process. These anomalies can range from misaligned dies to worn dies and even the presence of foreign objects within the minting chamber.

Their one-of-a-kind imperfections are what sets error coins apart and captures the attention of collectors. Some of the most prevalent coin-minting errors include (The Coin Collector, 2019):

- **Off-center strikes:** Coins not centered on the planchet, resulting in a coin with one edge raised and the other sunken.
- **Double strikes:** Coins subjected to the strikes of the dies twice, leading to a coin adorned with two sets of images and lettering.
- **Broadstrikes:** Coins struck without a collar, resulting in a raised edge encircling the entire circumference, as the planchet was not contained. Note that broadstrikes are often also off-centered.
- **Overdates:** Coins bearing incorrect dates, often due to die mistakes.
- **Mules:** Coins born from the accidental marriage of two different dies, featuring the wrong design on one side.

Below are examples of double strikes and off-center strikes:

The allure of error coins lies in their intriguing anomalies and their potential rarity and value. The worth of error coins hinges on several factors, including the type of error, the coin's denomination, and its production date. The most expensive error coins include the following (Millman, 2023):

- **The 1943 copper Lincoln cent:** A rare and valuable error coin made of copper instead of steel during WWII. Few exist, and they sell for millions. They have different names and mint marks, such as the unique 1943-D.
- **The 1937 three-legged buffalo nickel:** An off-center strike resulted in a buffalo depicted with only three legs. A scarcity of five known specimens makes each worth hundreds of thousands of dollars.
- **The 1942/1 overdate mercury dime:** This coin features an overdate, displaying the date 1942/1. Only a few hundred of these coins are known to exist, with each commanding tens of thousands of dollars.

For those intrigued by error coins and looking to identify and acquire them, here are some valuable tips:

- **Familiarize yourself with error types:** Delve into the diverse world of coin-minting errors. A solid understanding will enable you to identify these unique coins when they cross your path.
- **Examine coins closely:** Scrutinize coins for any imperfections. Watch for telltale signs such as off-center strikes, double strikes, broadstrikes, overdates, and mules.

- **Buy from reputable dealers:** Ensure your error coins are authentic by purchasing them from reputable dealers who can verify their authenticity.

With these insights, you will be better equipped to navigate the captivating realm of error coins. In this domain, every imperfection tells a story, and each discovery promises to uncover a numismatic treasure.

## DELVING DEEPER INTO THE ENIGMATIC WORLD OF PATTERN AND TRIAL COINS

Numismatics has many interesting aspects, and among them stands the category of pattern and trial coins. Often shrouded in mystery, these specimens represent experimental or prototype coins meticulously crafted by official mints.

The primary purpose of these coins is to serve as testing grounds for new designs, compositions, and manufacturing techniques (*Pattern coins*, 2017). Although these coins were never meant for everyday circulation, they found their way into the hands of government officials, mint employees, and, eventually, collectors.

The allure of pattern and trial coins to collectors can be attributed to many factors. Firstly, their scarcity and singularity contribute significantly to their desirability. Due to their experimental nature, only a few designs are typically manufactured, rendering them rare and highly sought after.

Secondly, they offer a window into the creative processes underlying coin design, providing insights into the evolutionary journey of specific coin series. Lastly, some of these coins are crafted from precious metals such as gold and silver, enhancing their numismatic value and providing them with intrinsic worth.

## THE INTRIGUING WORLD OF COLLECTING EXPERIMENTAL COIN DESIGNS AND PROTOTYPES

Venturing into the world of collecting pattern and trial coins is a journey ripe with excitement and intrigue. However, it is imperative to embark on this quest with knowledge, given the diversity within this category and the significant variation in their value. Factors like design, rarity, and condition are pivotal in determining their worth.

Numismatic history is punctuated with remarkable discoveries of pattern coins, each bearing its unique narrative (Yeoman et al., 2018):

- **The 1836 Gobrecht Dollar:** Revered as one of the rarest and most valuable pattern coins globally, this coin enjoys a place of honor in the numismatic world. Only a select few specimens are known to exist, and their valuation soars into the millions.
- **The 1913 Liberty Head Nickel:** Holding the distinction of being one of the rarest pattern coins, the 1913 Liberty Head Nickel commands attention. With only five known specimens in existence, each valued at a

lofty sum, this coin was never released into circulation due to its groundbreaking design.

Pattern and trial coins, with their aura of mystique and rarity, capture the imagination and kindle a fervor for collecting. Their uniqueness, scarcity, and intrinsic value make them prized treasures in the world of numismatics. If you aspire to venture into the realm of collecting these enigmatic coins, arm yourself with research and seek reputable dealers to guide you through this intriguing journey.

## CASE STUDY: THE QUEST FOR THE HOLY GRAIL COIN

Louis Eliasberg was a renowned coin collector with a remarkable goal: To assemble a complete collection of every coin issued by the United States Mint. He achieved this feat in 1950, becoming the first and only person to do so. However, his journey took work, especially when it came to acquiring one of the rarest and most coveted coins in American history: the 1822 Half Eagle.

Only three specimens are known to exist today, and two are permanently housed in the Smithsonian Institution (*Louis Eliasberg*, 2021). The third one is the only example available for private ownership, and it has a fascinating provenance that traces back to some of the earliest and most influential coin collectors in the US.

This is where Louis Eliasberg enters the picture. Eliasberg was a successful banker and a passionate coin collector who started his hobby in 1925. He envisioned building a complete collection of US coins and spared no expense or effort in pursuing this dream. He bought entire collections from other collectors and dealers and attended numerous auctions and sales. He also hired experts and consultants to help him locate and identify the rarest and most elusive coins—the 1822 Half Eagle being the Holy Grail.

After almost 20 years of searching, in 1945, Eliasberg learned that an anonymous collector had an 1822 Half Eagle for sale. He immediately contacted them and negotiated a deal. He paid $14,000 for the coin, a huge sum at the time (*Louis Eliasberg*, 2021). He later said that he would have paid twice as much if necessary. With this purchase, Eliasberg completed his collection of US gold coins, and he became the first person to own every coin issued by the US Mint.

The story of Louis Eliasberg and his pursuit of the 1822 Half Eagle is a captivating case study of a collector's passion and determination. He faced many challenges and obstacles in his quest for this numismatic masterpiece but never gave up or settled for less. He dedicated his time, money, and energy to achieve his goal and eventually succeeded. His story inspires all coin collectors who aspire to own history's rarest and most beautiful coins.

9

# COINS AS HISTORICAL TREASURES

I magine a coin as a time capsule, a tiny vessel carrying a message from the past. When we hold a coin in our hands, we are connecting with the people of the past.

We can imagine the hands that have touched it, the markets where it has been exchanged, and the stories it could tell if it could speak. Each coin has its own unique story—who made it, who carried it around, and what it symbolized for them.

Interacting with the people and events that helped to form our world is like having a secret window into the past. Think of coin collecting as something similar to archaeology, except instead of working in the mud, you are looking into the daily routines of those who lived in the past.

It's an opportunity to delve into human history's astounding diversity and reveal the beauty tucked away in these tiny, artistic treasures.

124 | THOMAS KNOLLS

## STORIES WITHIN COINS

These shiny bits of metal we often take for granted are like tiny time capsules that hold incredible stories of bygone eras and diverse cultures. Coins are reflections of the cultures and societies that created them. They depict the rulers, deities, and symbols important to the people of the time. Coins can also tell us about the economic and political conditions of a particular era. A coin from ancient Rome might depict the emperor on one side and a goddess of victory on the other.

For instance, take the Brutus "Eid Mar" denarius, a coin that commemorates the assassination of Julius Caesar (*Denarius of Brutus*, n.d.). It boasts a portrait of Brutus, one of the conspirators, and a pileus (cap of liberty) flanked by daggers on the reverse. This coin symbolizes the liberation of the Roman Republic from dictatorship, marking a pivotal moment in history.

A coin from the Middle Ages might depict a king or queen on one side and a cross on the other, suggesting the prominence of Christianity during this period. Coins also reflect cultural and political shifts. The Athens decadrachm, for instance, celebrates Greece's victory over Persia and features Athena and an owl on one side, symbolizing wisdom, vigilance, and civic pride. The inscription "Athens" hints at the city-state's dominance during its Golden Age (Shutterly, 2023). Historians use texts, archaeological findings, and iconographic analysis to decode these symbols. Expert sources like *Coin World* and *The Numismatist* further illuminate coin context and meaning. Coins also impact our understanding of history when discovered.

Coin discoveries offer us a remarkable glimpse into history and the cultures of days gone by. Let's travel back to 1992 when a jaw-dropping find in England unveiled over 15,000 Roman coins from the 3rd century AD (Haughton, 2016). It's like peering into the ancient economic life of Roman Britain through the lens of numismatics.

But these coin discoveries are not just dusty relics; they are history's storytellers. In 2016, a collection of silver coins emerged in Israel, dating back to the Bar Kokhba Revolt, a 2nd-century AD Jewish uprising against the Roman Empire (Hasson, 2016). This find shed new light on the rebellion and revealed that Jewish rebels had their own currency—a powerful testament to their fight for independence.

So, when we chance upon these coin treasures, it's not just a delightful historical tidbit; it is like assembling a grand jigsaw puzzle of our past, one coin at a time. Every corner of the globe boasts its own captivating coin tales, offering a glimpse into the richness of human history.

Imagine traveling back to 600 BC in what's now Turkey, where the very first known coins were minted in the kingdom of Lydia. The people crafted these coins from electrum, a natural blend of gold and silver. Among them, the Lydian Lion stands out, showcasing a majestic lion on one side and a bull's head on the other, like ancient art in your pocket.

China's numismatic history runs deep with the Chinese cash, a design that endured for over two millennia, from the 11th century BC to the 20th century AD. This unique coin features a circular shape with a square hole at its center, often strung on cords and worn as fashionable jewelry, adding a touch of monetary bling to everyday life.

Set sail to the 16th century and the Spanish doubloon, a golden treasure that traversed the globe in trade and swashbuckling pirate tales. These coins still bewitch collectors today, prized not only for their historical significance but also for their captivating beauty.

These are just a sneak peek of the countless coin narratives gracing our world. Coins are more than just currency; they are portals to bygone eras. Through their study, we unravel the stories of cultures, economies, and societies long gone, reminding us that history isn't just found in textbooks; sometimes, it is right in the palm of your hand.

## THE ARTISTRY OF COIN DESIGN

Coins are more than just currency; they are also works of art. Coin designers have used their skills to create miniature masterpieces that celebrate cultures, commemorate events, and honor esteemed individuals. This is the art of coin design, a fusion of currency and culture that has evolved over the centuries. It has changed dramatically over time, reflecting the artistic trends and innovations of each period.

The bimetallic monetary standard of the Achaemenid Empire (550–330 BCE) was a system of currency that used two metals, gold and silver, as legal tender. The Persian Daric was a gold coin that was worth 20 silver Siglos. The Daric and the Siglos were widely accepted throughout the Achaemenid Empire, stretching from India to the Mediterranean Sea. The Daric was introduced by Darius the Great (521–486 BC) and quickly became known throughout the ancient world for its remarkable purity of gold (*Persian Daric*, n.d.).

In ancient Greece and Rome, coin designers embraced realism and detail, creating stunning portraits of gods, goddesses, emperors, and heroes. The tetradrachm of Athens, for example, depicts the goddess Athena and her sacred owl with remarkable precision and elegance. The Middle Ages saw a shift to more abstract and stylized designs, influenced by Christianity and feudalism (*Origins of coins*, n.d.).

Coins often bore crosses, saints, or heraldic symbols, such as the fleur-de-lis on French coins or the rose on English ones. The Renaissance brought a revival of classical art and humanism, inspiring coin designers to create intricate and elaborate designs with elements like columns, statues, and laurel wreaths. The florin of Florence, for example, features a lily on one side and John the Baptist on the other, representing the city's patron saint and economic prosperity. In our modern era, coin designers use various techniques and technologies to create diverse and innovative designs. As we discussed earlier, some rely on traditional methods like engraving and sculpting, while others use digital tools like 3D modeling and laser cutting (*A modern Britannia*, n.d.).

Regardless of their chosen technique, coin designers must meticulously contemplate every facet of their creations. Symbols, imagery, and inscriptions are carefully selected to convey their intended message. For instance, a recurring theme in coin design is the portrayal of rulers and leaders. These images serve as a potent means to communicate authority, ideology, and legacy. Consider the portrait of Queen Elizabeth II on British coins, symbolizing stability and tradition. In contrast, the portrait of Mao Zedong on coins from the People's Republic of China is a powerful emblem of communism and revolution. Some coin designs feature iconic images that have transcended leadership, like George Washington's portrait on the United States dollar bill—a globally recognized profile.

Coins also double as historical chronicles. Their inscriptions and imagery weave tales of momentous events, pay tribute to exceptional individuals, and celebrate diverse cultures. For example, the United States Mint releases commemorative coins annually to mark pivotal moments in American history. In 2023, they honored the 50th anniversary of the Apollo 11 moon landing with a coin that features an astronaut's footprint on the lunar surface. Across the border, the Canadian Mint's *Wildlife* series captures the essence of Canadian fauna, from the moose to the polar bear and the industrious beaver. Coins also serve as guardians of cultural narratives and historical epochs. The coins of ancient Greece and Rome, for instance, provide invaluable insights into the societies and the ethos' of those eras.

Coin design is not just a craft; it's an exquisite art form. It is where designers channel their talents to create miniature marvels that pay homage to cultures, commemorate the past, and salute exceptional people. Coins transcend their monetary value; they are canvases that convey stories and safeguard

history, making them more than just currency—they are historical artifacts and works of art. The next time you hold a coin in
your hand, take a moment to appreciate its beauty and meaning. You might be surprised by what you discover.

## THE ROLE OF NUMISMATIC DETECTIVES

Have you ever wondered what stories lie behind the coins in
your pocket? The allure of archaeological coin finds is undeniable. The prospect of unearthing a buried treasure trove of
ancient coins is enough to set the heart of any numismatist
racing.

One of the most exciting aspects of numismatics is the possi-
bility of finding coins that have been buried or lost for
centuries. These coins can reveal secrets about the past, such as
the location of ancient cities, the identity of rulers, or the trade
routes of civilizations. Some of the most notable discoveries
that rewrote history through coins include:

1. **The Hoxne Hoard:** A massive stash of Roman gold and
   silver coins, jewelry, and other objects found by a metal
   detectorist in England in 1992. The hoard dates from
   the late 4th and early 5th centuries AD and provides
   insights into the end of Roman Britain (Haughton,
   2016).
2. **Sylloge Nummorum Graecorum:** A monumental
   project that catalogs and illustrates all the known Greek
   coins from antiquity to the present day. The project
   began in 1931 and is still ongoing, with thousands of

volumes published by various institutions worldwide. The SNG has helped scholars and collectors identify and classify Greek coins from different regions and periods (*Sylloge Nummorum Graecorum*, n.d.).

3. **The Shipwreck of the SS Central America:** An 1857 hurricane-related sinking of a steamship off the coast of North Carolina, carrying tons of gold coins and bars from California. The wreck was discovered in 1988, and the coins were recovered over several expeditions, yielding rare and valuable gold specimens from the California Gold Rush era (Liberatore, 2022).

Once a coin is discovered, numismatic detectives begin their work. They investigate the provenance and lineage of the coin, seeking to unravel its mysteries.

Numismatists use a variety of techniques to trace the origins and journeys of coins. They examine the coin's metal composition, design, and inscriptions. They also consult historical records and other experts.

By piecing together the clues, numismatists can reconstruct the coin's journey through time and space. They can learn about the people who used it, the places it traveled, and the events it witnessed.

For example, a numismatist might discover that an ancient Roman coin was minted in Rome, shipped to Britain, and then buried by a Roman soldier during the Boudican revolt of 60 AD.

Although it can be difficult, tracing the beginnings and adventures of coins can be very gratifying. Numismatic detectives play a vital role in preserving and interpreting our numismatic heritage.

Sometimes, coin collectors don't have to go far to find valuable and rare coins. They can stumble upon them in unexpected places, such as flea markets, garage sales, or even their own change. These serendipitous encounters can result in amazing rewards for those who know what to look for. Some examples of coin collectors who made incredible finds are:

- **Don Lutes Jr.:** A Massachusetts teenager who found a 1943 copper penny in his school cafeteria change in 1947. The penny was one of only a handful mistakenly struck in copper instead of steel during World War II when copper was needed for ammunition. The penny was sold at an auction for $204,000 in 2019 (Neuendorf, 2019).
- **The Walton specimen:** Melva Givens, sister to coin enthusiast George Walton, unwittingly possessed one of the five 1913 Liberty Head nickels, never officially minted by the US Mint. In 1962, she inherited it after her brother's fatal car crash. Unrecognized as genuine, it collected dust in her closet for over 40 years. In 1992, Melva passed away, leaving it to her family, who struggled to prove its authenticity. In 2003, experts at a Baltimore coin convention confirmed its worth of $2.5 million, dubbing it the "Walton specimen." The family kept it as an heirloom, lending it to museums. Finally,

in 2018, it sold at auction for a staggering $4.5 million, ranking among the most expensive coins ever sold. Melva Givens' tale epitomizes hidden coin histories and unexpected values, a testament to her family's perseverance and her brother's enduring passion (*Rare liberty head*, 2013).

## BONUS ACTIVITY: HISTORICAL COIN REENACTMENT

Historical coin reenactments are a fun and educational way to learn about the role of coins in history. By recreating historical transactions or events using coins from the relevant time period, participants can gain a deeper understanding of coins' economic and cultural significance. It could be an excellent idea to bring up to a collecting club leader, as it allows collectors to share their passions and get to know one another better.

Here are some ideas for historical coin reenactments (*Reenactment*, n.d.):

1. **Reenact a historical event:** For example, you could reenact a Roman coin auction or a medieval trade fair.
2. **Create a historical coin scavenger hunt:** Hide coins from the relevant time period around a designated area and have participants search for them.
3. **Dress up in period clothing:** This will help to create a more immersive and entertaining experience for participants.

4. **Use historical props:** This could include market stalls, trade goods, and even weapons (if you reenact a historical battle).

5. **Explain the historical context of the reenactment to participants:** This will help them to understand the significance of the activities they are participating in.

6. **Encourage participants to ask questions:** This is a great way to learn more about the history of coins and their role in society.

Historical coin reenactments can be a valuable tool for teaching students about history and economics. They can also be a fun and rewarding activity for adults of all ages.

# 10

# EXPLORING NUMISMATIC ARTISTRY AND DESIGN

One fateful Thanksgiving day remains vividly in my memory despite the passing years. I was around the rebellious age of 15 or 16, and it was the day my grandfather allowed me to hold my great-grandfather's age-old pine tree shilling. This event was a surreal experience, akin to clutching a tangible piece of living history itself. The weight of the coin in my palm bore an unexpected sense of reassurance—and my curious fingers danced gently across the elaborate patterns and cryptic symbols etched meticulously on both sides.

As I cautiously shifted the coin, allowing the play of light to grace its surface, an enchanting spectacle unfolded before my eyes. The coin seemed to harbor an enigmatic universe within. Its shiny façade conjured a spellbinding ballet of ever-changing hues and textures. It was like the coin guarded a trove of concealed secrets and untold tales, beckoning my inquisitive spirit into its unfathomable depths.

My imagination soared to dizzying heights as I conjured up vivid scenarios, envisioning the myriad of narratives and mysteries this ancient artifact might hold close to its metallic heart. My fascination knew no bounds.

At that moment, I found myself utterly captivated by the idea of the masterful hands that had crafted this coin. The notion of the countless moments it had silently observed, like a stoic sentinel standing guard throughout its extraordinary journey through the hallways of history, left me in a state of profound reverence.

To me, that unassuming coin transcended its metallic existence; it emerged as a tangible stargate to an alternate cosmos, teeming with history uncharted and connections concealed— all conspiring to be unveiled in the most extraordinary ways.

## THE EVOLUTION OF COIN ARTISTRY

The history of coin artistry unfurls over an astonishing expanse of 2,500 years, weaving an intricate web that pulsates with the heartbeat of human civilization's ever-evolving saga (*Origins of coins*, n.d.). These ancient artifacts, etched with designs that transcend temporal boundaries, emerge as manufactured fossils. They resonate with the essence of cultures, politics, and technological marvels. This unique craft, an exquisite fusion of functionality and aesthetics, has been intricately woven into human history. It has left its imprint across the ever-shifting landscapes of time and geography.

Our odyssey commences around the 7th century BC, enveloped within the heartland of Lydia—nestled in what we now call modern-day Turkey. Here, the ancients sowed the budding seeds of coinage. Forged from electrum, these early coins bore designs that, though outwardly unassuming, concealed profound layers of symbolism. Geometric patterns, cryptic symbols, and the enigmatic visages of animals whispered cryptic tales of bygone eras. Yet, the weighty countenance of authority—a seal denoting weight and value—set these Lydian coins apart (*Origins of coins*, n.d.).

The Greeks were the first to infuse a rich vein of artistic expression into the very soul of coin design. No longer were coins mere vessels of exchange; they became canvases upon which the artworks of religious devotion, cultural identity, and artistic genius developed. These small metal disks bore silent witness to the appearances of gods and goddesses, heroes and heroines, mythical creatures, and the flora and fauna that adorned the Greek landscape. Rulers, monumental milestones of history, and architectural wonders leaped from the coin's surface. A bubbly realism garnered them acclaim for their unparalleled beauty.

The torch of coin artistry was subsequently passed to the Romans, who rekindled its flames with their distinctive touch. Roman coins radiated an unassailable uniformity and standardization that set them apart as beacons in the ancient world. Roman coins evolved into formidable instruments of propaganda and communication. With their coinage, emperors could cast their messages to the farthest reaches of their sprawling empire. Emperors and sweeping social reforms materialized on these exquisite disks in dazzling splendor. The spread of Roman coins transcended geographical boundaries, influencing the coinage of far-off lands, including the Celtic, Germanic, and Byzantine cultures (*Origins of coins*, n.d.).

As history unraveled the scroll into the medieval era, the cadence of coin artistry was muted. Political fragmentation, economic upheaval, and cultural stagnation in Europe culminated in coin designs of stark simplicity. Many coins of this period bore nothing more than a solitary cross or monogram on one side—with the reverse graced by little more than a name or title. Yet, occasional stars gleamed in the night sky in this apparent artistic dormancy. The Byzantine Empire steadfastly preserved the Roman tradition by embellishing coins with portraits of emperors and religious iconography (Markowitz, 2022).

The Renaissance era ushered in a rebirth of coin artistry in Europe, mirroring the broader cultural revival of the age. Inspired by the grandeur of classical antiquity, the tenets of humanism, and the force of naturalism, coin design embraced expressive artistry. Rulers, saints, patrons, artists, scholars, and luminaries from diverse walks of life found their immortal visages gracing these exquisite coins. Scenes drawn from mythology, history, literature, art, science, and religion whirled across the coin's surface, captivating admirers with an exquisite blend of opulence and monetary value (Stevens, 2023).

The modern era unveiled a fresh chapter in coin artistry. Seismic political revolutions, relentless industrial innovations, and ceaseless cultural movements forged this chapter. Coin designs burgeoned in complexity, diversity, and provocation. Artists eagerly embraced novel themes, symbols, colors, shapes, and materials. They used their creations as mirrors to reflect the ever-metamorphosing world. Modern coins surged with life, representing leaders, movements, ideologies, and triumphs. The imagery offered a vivid reflection of the intricate complexities of contemporary society (Coins, 2023).

Among the pantheon of American coin artists, five luminaries burn with an incandescent brilliance, their influence profound and their talents transcendent (*Five famous*, 2022):

1. **Adolph A. Weinman:** The brilliant mind behind the iconic Winged Liberty Head dime, more commonly known as the Mercury Dime, and the Walking Liberty Half Dollar. His work is celebrated for its exquisite and lifelike depictions of Liberty.

2. **James Earle Fraser:** The creative genius responsible for the evocative Buffalo Nickel, whose inspiration flowed from his encounters with Native Americans and the sprawling American West.

3. **Augustus Saint-Gaudens:** Renowned for the ethereal Double Eagle, which is considered one of the most exquisite coins ever to grace the world's mints. This masterpiece portrays Liberty striding forward, carrying a torch and olive branch, while a soaring eagle graces the reverse. This coin stands as my personal favorite, so much so that I have chosen to feature it on the cover of this book.

4. **Charles Barber:** The master engraver behind the Barber dime, quarter, and half dollar coins that enjoyed wide circulation for a quarter of a century. His designs featured a classical bust of Liberty, adorned with a cap and wreath, while a heraldic eagle adorned the reverse.

5. **Christian Gobrecht:** The visionary who introduced the enduring Seated Liberty design, adorning various denominations for over half a century. His designs featured a seated Liberty holding a shield and a pole with a cap, with varying reverse designs based on the coin.

These five luminaries played pivotal roles in shaping designs that continue to enrapture, forging a bridge between their era and the generations yet to come.

Coin artistry, a captivating field of study, stands as a portal through the passage of time, culture, and values across diverse societies. It emerges as a profound form of artistic expression, a canvas upon which artists and engravers display their boundless talents, creativity, and innovation. Coin artistry, at its core, serves as a testament to the enduring allure and significance of coins—weaving a bridge between the pragmatic realm of currency and the ethereal realm of art.

## SYMBOLISM AND STORYTELLING THROUGH COINS

Beyond their function as mere conduits for economic transactions, coins serve a deeper purpose—fostering a symbiotic union between artistic expression and effective communication.

They assume the mantle of master narrators, grand authors of tales, and bearers of profound symbolism. They are reflective portals, mirroring the kaleidoscope of human existence, history, culture, values, and identity. Coins ascend to the peak of their potential, assuming the mantle of potent vessels for the art of storytelling. They bear the transformative power to inspire, enlighten, commemorate, and exalt the human condition.

The realm of fauna and flora, frequently adorning coins, assumes the mantle of environmental ambassadors. These motifs convey the intrinsic attributes of these life forms and articulate a broader message about the importance of preserving the natural world.

On Australian coins, the kangaroo symbolizes the nation's extraordinary fauna, the majesty of its landscapes, and the rich heritage that intertwines with nature. The majestic eagle, gracing American currency, signifies the nation's fortitude and independence and serves as a clarion call to patriotic fervor. In stark contrast, the lotus adorning Chinese coins encapsulates lofty ideals of beauty and the harmonious existence cherished by Chinese culture (*World coins*, 2023).

Another recurring motif—ubiquitous in its presence—is the emblem signifying a nation. Within this design lies the quintessence of a people's identity, a wellspring of unity and diversity. For instance, the iconic maple leaf adorning Canadian coinage—a resounding emblem of Canada's breathtaking natural magnificence. Similarly, the star and crescent that embellish Turkish coins stand as steadfast sentinels, bearing witness to Turkey's Islamic faith. Meanwhile, the euro emblem, delicately etched upon European currency, embodies the profound synergy of economic integration and stands as a testament to the collaborative partnership and the unyielding bond between the diverse nations of Europe.

None can compete with the portrayal of luminous figures among the motifs adorning these masterpieces (*World coins*, 2023). This motif, steeped in profound symbolism, extends into the realms of legitimacy and authority. Yet, it is not limited to this. It becomes a conduit encapsulating the very essence of the persona depicted. The regal visage of Queen Elizabeth II etched upon British coinage stands as an emblem of sovereignty and the exceptional character she exhibited as the head of state and the Commonwealth during her reign.

Conversely, Abraham Lincoln's visage etched onto U.S. currency serves as an evocative emblem, a reminder of wise leadership, courageous undertakings during the turbulent Civil War, and a beacon of emancipation from the shackles of slavery. Similarly, the likeness of Mahatma Gandhi adorning Indian rupees is an eternal symbol of unwavering commitment to nonviolence, an embodiment of peace, and the relentless struggle for freedom from the shackles of British oppression.

Another recurrent theme etched upon numismatic master-pieces is the depiction of scenes or events (*World coins, 2023*). This is an immersive narrative imbued with historical or contemporary importance. Take, for instance, the portrayal of Apollo 11's lunar voyage etched upon U.S. coinage. It is a symbol of extraordinary scientific dominance, an embodiment of the unquenchable spirit of exploration, and a testament to human ingenuity reaching its pinnacle. Conversely, the German government somberly immortalizes the fall of the Berlin Wall on their coins. The imaging serves as a poignant testament to Germany's political metamorphosis, the journey toward reunification, and the eternal yearning for liberty.

## CONTEMPORARY TRENDS IN COIN DESIGN

Coin design, as an ever-evolving discipline, reflects the dynamism and complexities of the modern world. Today's coin designers find themselves in a delicate balancing act, juggling the demands of tradition, functionality, security, and aesthetics, all while embracing innovation and cutting-edge technology in their pursuit of numismatic artistry. Coin collectors of the present era are privy to a vast spectrum of coins that serve as eloquent expressions of creative diversity.

One of the most conspicuous and striking trends in contempo-rary coin design is the bold utilization of color. Color is a potent tool that infuses coins with vitality, realism, and stark contrast, lending layers of meaning and evoking a symphony of emotions. The application of color to coins spans an array of techniques, including pad printing, laser frosting, enamel coating, and holographic foils. A noteworthy example of this colorful coin manifestation is Canadian glow-in-the-dark dinosaur coins (Hornyak, 2011).

Another captivating facet of contemporary coin design embraces the unconventional in terms of shape and materials. Once bound to the circular and metallic confines, coins have broken free from these traditional limitations. They now don the garb of squares, triangles, polygons, or even hearts. Furthermore, coins defy the status quo by manifesting in materials as diverse as wood, glass, ceramic, or plastic. A prime example is the refreshingly innovative Fiji Coca-Cola bottle cap coins (*Buy gold*, 2023).

Yet another riveting dimension of modern coin design revolves around interactivity and mobility. Coins are no longer static artifacts but dynamic canvases with elements that can spin, flip, tilt, or pull to unveil concealed features or invoke mesmerizing effects. Some coins even harbor embedded magnets, springs, or gears, inviting collectors to partake in puzzles, games, and intricate mechanical marvels. This dimension comes to life in the Mongolian Wildlife Protection series, where coin components come to life through interactive elements (*Mongolian gobi bear*, n.d.).

With its myriad facets, coin design is a captivating and diverse discipline, offering a boundless playground for artistic expression and groundbreaking innovation. For contemporary coin collectors, it is an invitation to immerse yourself in the aesthetic and conceptual kaleidoscope that embodies the current trends in coin design. Beyond being a mere medium of exchange, coin design emerges as an art form that weaves together history, culture, and the ever-advancing frontiers of human creativity.

## CASE STUDY: DESIGNING A NUMISMATIC MASTERPIECE

In contemporary numismatic artistry emerge paragons of design innovation. The Canadian 2017 $25 Fine Silver Coin —The Great Trail is one such coin. It is an ode to Canada's monumental feat—creating the world's most extensive network of recreational trails. It is an unrivaled numismatic masterpiece, an intricate cohesion of engraving, selective coloration, and micro-texture. It renders a cartographic mastery mirroring the trail's sprawling complexity. Yet, this coin's groundbreaking design extends further. It defies numismatic conventions with its unique shape, tracing the contours of Canada's borders, etching itself into the pages of coin design history.

Guiding this artistic odyssey is Steve Hepburn, a graphic designer and illustrator whose storied collaboration with the Royal Canadian Mint has left a permanent mark. Hepburn's inspiration sprouted from a genuine desire to encapsulate Canada's breathtaking natural grandeur, stunning landscapes, and indomitable spirit of exploration and adventure. He didn't merely seek to craft a coin but an experiential artwork that would transport individuals along the trail's meandering path. Most significantly, Hepburn harbored the aspiration of redefining the essence of coinage, pushing the boundaries of design and production to forge something truly exceptional.

Hepburn's creativity commenced with an immersive exploration of the Great Trail—delving into its rural and wilderness landscapes—which artfully unite Canada's 13 provinces and territories. Informed by this comprehensive research, he sketched many concepts, boldly experimenting with the coin's shape, layout, and color palette. His vision crystallized into a map-like design, an intricate portrayal of the trail's course across Canada. Selective coloration emerged as a tool to accentuate the distinct regions and environments adorning the trail. Hepburn meticulously integrated micro-textured labels for major cities, landmarks, and bodies of water. He chose an exuberant palette of colors, poised to strike a harmonious contrast against the coin's silver backdrop, invoking depth and dimension.

The culmination of Hepburn's imaginative brainchild yielded a final design. The coin was submitted to the Royal Canadian Mint for approval and eventual production. The Mint, captivated by Hepburn's innovative vision and artistic prowess, pledged to employ its advanced technology and unwavering craftsmanship in bringing the design to life. A cutting machine assumed the task of crafting a master tool, meticulously shaping the coin's distinctive outline. A laser-engraving machine was enlisted to create a master die, transferring the design's intricate engravings onto each pristine blank. A pad-printing machine bestowed the coin with its selective coloration. Finally, a micro-engraving machine lent a security feature, manifesting as a maple leaf-shaped privy mark, concealing the year "2017."

A limited number of 5,500 coins, each bearing a face value of $25 and weighing 1.5oz, were released (*2017 $25 fine silver coin,* n.d.). These numismatic gems were gracefully ensconced within black clamshell cases, their exteriors adorned with a graphic beauty box that showcased Hepburn's original artwork. The Mint provided a certificate of authenticity to accompany each coin, allowing collectors access to comprehensive details concerning the coin's design, specifications, mintage, and unique serial number.

# 11

# UNVEILING COIN COLLECTING
# LEGENDS

What do Nicolas Cage, King Farouk of Egypt, J.P. Morgan, David Beckham, and Neil Armstrong have in common? They are all members of the extraordinary fellowship of coin collectors.

Coin collectors may be drawn to coins because of their worth, beauty, or historical significance. However, a few numismatics enthusiasts have gone above and beyond the norm to achieve legendary status. They have gathered amazing collections, made astounding discoveries, and significantly impacted science.

## LEGENDARY COLLECTORS AND THEIR STORIES: PIONEERS OF NUMISMATICS

Numismatics is much more than a pastime. It is a way of exploring history, culture, and art through the medium of money. But who were the people who started this fascinating pursuit? Who were the pioneers of numismatics?

### Francesco Petrarch

Petrarch was a luminary of the Renaissance, renowned for his scholarship, poetry, and humanist ideals. However, he possessed another facet of his intellectual pursuits—a fervent passion for ancient coins, mainly bronze Roman ones (Victor, 2015).

His humanistic studies kindled Petrarch's venture into the world of numismatics. To him, studying these ancient coins was a portal to understanding the profound opulence of Roman history, culture, and art. He also harbored the belief that the collection of these coins played a vital role in safeguarding the Roman legacy for generations yet unborn.

In his era, his coin collection was a marvel, one of the largest and most prestigious of its kind. His quest for these relics led him to traverse the length and breadth of Italy and Europe, a testament to his dedication. His correspondence with fellow numismatists and scholars facilitated the exchange of invaluable information and coins.

For Petrarch, his coin collection was more than a personal indulgence; it was an indispensable tool for his scholarly pursuits. With these ancient artifacts in hand, he delved into the annals of Roman history, peered into their religion's depths, and examined their art's intricacies. His writings on numismatics, including the *Epistola ad Lucam de Penna* (Letter to Luca de Penna) and the *De Viris Illustribus* (On Illustrious Men), stand as pillars in the discipline (Victor, 2015).

His work in numismatics marked a turning point in its development. He was among the first to approach the study of Roman coins systematically, using them as a lens to reconstruct the mosaic of Roman history and culture. His pioneering efforts laid the foundation for the modern study of numismatics.

Even today, Petrarch's legacy as a numismatist endures. His prized coin collection resides in the Biblioteca Ambrosiana in Milan, Italy, where it continues to inspire scholars from across the globe. His works on numismatics remain vital resources consulted by modern-day numismatists.

In Petrarch, we find a numismatist and a true polymath whose insatiable intellectual curiosity left an indelible mark, contributing significantly to the Renaissance's burgeoning intellect and spirit.

## Jean Foy-Vaillant

Let's delve into the 17th-century world of Jean Foy-Vaillant, an exceptional French lawyer who defied convention and emerged as a true pioneer in the captivating realm of ancient coins (Khounani, 2021). This numismatist was ahead of his time. But hold on; his story doesn't stop there. He's also celebrated as a collector extraordinaire and the esteemed guardian of coins at the Royal Museum of France.

But what fueled this passionate obsession for numismatics in the heart of Jean Foy-Vaillant? We need to explore his deep engagement with humanist studies to unearth the roots of this fascination. He held a steadfast belief that ancient coins were like time capsules, capable of unveiling the long-forgotten chapters of history, the subtleties of culture, and the exquisite artistry of antiquity. For him, coin collecting transcended the realm of mere hobby; it was a noble mission dedicated to preserving the treasures of the ancient world for the generations yet to come.

However, Jean Foy-Vaillant was far from content with a sedentary scholarly existence. He embarked on audacious adventures across the vast expanses of Europe and Asia, crisscrossing continents in relentless pursuit of new additions to his ever-expanding coin treasury. Yet, he was no solitary explorer; he forged strong bonds with fellow coin enthusiasts and scholars, engaging in vibrant exchanges of knowledge and coins. He also carried the weighty responsibility of representing the French government on various missions, acquiring coins that would enrich the collections of the Royal Museum. With unwavering dedication, he meticulously compiled a comprehensive catalog of Roman imperial coins, ensuring their historical significance would endure for posterity.

Jean Foy-Vaillant didn't simply amass these coins as lifeless artifacts. Instead, he wielded them as potent instruments for scholarly exploration. His collection served as an invaluable gateway to unlocking the mysteries of ancient history, the intricacies of religious practices, and the evolution of artistic expression. And that's not all; he left an indelible mark on the world of numismatics through his written works, including *Arsacidarum Imperium* and *Achaemenidarum Imperium*—seminal texts that delve into the captivating histories of Parthian and Persian coins (Khounani, 2021).

Jean Foy-Vaillant's pioneering work cast a lasting shadow on the evolution of numismatics. He was among the earliest scholars to approach the systematic study of ancient coins, recognizing their pivotal role as essential puzzle pieces in reconstructing the intricate tapestry of ancient civilizations. His contributions laid the foundation upon which the modern field of numismatics now proudly stands.

In modernity, the legacy of Jean Foy-Vaillant as a numismatist continues to shine brightly. His remarkable coin collection has found a cherished home within the hallowed halls of the Biblioteca Ambrosiana in Milan, Italy, drawing scholars from all corners of the globe who seek to decipher its enigmatic stories (Khounani, 2021). And those invaluable works on numismatics? They remain as treasured references, essential reading for today's passionate numismatists.

Jean Foy-Vaillant's enchantment with numismatics represents but one facet of his expansive intellectual curiosity. His contributions transcended the realm of coins, leaving an indelible mark on the Renaissance and the course of intellectual history itself.

## King Farouk of Egypt

King Farouk was the penultimate monarch of Egypt, who ruled from 1936 to 1952. He was known for his lavish lifestyle and love of collecting various objects, such as stamps, watches, jewels, and coins. He had one of the most impressive coin collections in the world, which included rare and valuable specimens from different countries and eras (Garrett, 2022).

His coin collection was estimated to have over 100,000 coins, which he acquired from various sources. He often bought coins from dealers who traveled to Egypt to sell him their inventory. He also sent agents to purchase coins from auctions and private collections in Europe and America. He even obtained some coins by dubious means, such as confiscating them from travelers or smuggling them out of museums.

Farouk's collection contained many remarkable pieces, such as the 1933 Saint-Gaudens double eagle, the silver dollar from 1804, and the Liberty Head nickel from 1913. He also had a complete set of $20 gold coins, a multitude of ancient Greek and Roman coins, and hundreds of pattern and proof coins. He displayed his coins in his palace in Cairo, where he enjoyed showing them to his guests and admirers (Bretz, 2015).

His numismatic escapades ended in 1952 when he was over-thrown by a military coup and forced to leave the country. The new government seized his coins and sold them at an auction in Cairo in 1954. The auction lasted for two weeks and attracted many buyers worldwide. The auction catalog listed almost 3,000 lots, but many more coins were sold without being cataloged or recorded. Some coins were stolen or lost during the auction process, while others were smuggled out of the country (Garrett, 2022).

The king's coin collection is still considered one of the most legendary collections in numismatic history. Many of his coins have found their way into other famous collections, such as the John J. Pittman Collection. Some of his coins have also set records at auctions, such as the 1933 Saint-Gaudens double eagle, which sold for over $18 million. King Farouk's coin collection is a testament to his passion for numismatics and his extravagant and controversial personality.

## MODERN ICONS AND TRAILBLAZERS

Many people, from history buffs to art lovers, collect coins as a hobby. Some of the most famous and influential figures world-wide are also avid coin collectors who have amassed impressive collections of rare and valuable coins. Next, we will examine some of the most notable celebrity coin collectors and their fascinating collections (*The most notable,* 2023):

## John Lennon

John Lennon was a singer-songwriter and a member of the iconic and successful band The Beatles. He was also a coin collector fascinated with ancient coins, especially those from India. He often dedicated extended periods to examining his collection, frequently displaying it to acquaintances and enthusiasts who dropped by his residence. Following Lennon's death in the 80s, Sotheby's in London auctioned his coin compilation. The collection, valued at approximately $10,000, encompassed almost 700 coins.

## Neil Armstrong

Neil Armstrong was not only the first man on the moon but also a passionate coin collector. He had a collection of coins related to his field of interest, such as commemorative coins honoring space missions, astronauts, and pilots. He also had some unique coins that he brought back from his lunar voyage, such as a silver dollar that he carried in his spacesuit pocket. Heritage Auctions auctioned his coin collection following Armstrong's passing in 2012. The collection, consisting of over 2,000 coins, was appraised to have a value exceeding $5 million.

## Jay Leno

Jay Leno is a comedian and former host of The Tonight Show, known for his love of cars and motorcycles. He is also a coin collector with a keen interest in ancient coins, especially those from the Roman Empire. He displays an extensive collection of

Roman coins in his garage alongside his vintage vehicles. The celebrity enjoys learning about the history and culture of the ancient world through his coins, and he often shares his knowledge and enthusiasm with his guests and viewers. Rare and unusual coins, such as an 1804 silver dollar and a 1913 Liberty Head nickel, are also part of his collection. He enjoys learning about the history and culture of the ancient world through his coins, and he often shares his knowledge and enthusiasm with his guests and viewers.

## Nicolas Cage

Nicolas Cage is an award-winning actor who starred in many blockbuster movies, including National Treasure, Face/Off, and Con Air. He is also a passionate coin collector who has spent millions of dollars on rare and historic coins. It's been rumored that he holds a 1933 Double Eagle, counted among the most precious coins ever produced, of which only 13 confirmed examples exist. His assortment is valued at over $10 million and encompasses some of the globe's most coveted coins, including a 1913 Liberty Head nickel and a 1792 silver center cent.

These are just some of the most notable celebrity coin collectors who have shown love and appreciation for coins. Coin collecting is a hobby that can enrich one's life with knowledge, beauty, and joy. Whether you are interested in history, art, or culture, there is a coin for you. You never know what treasures you might find when you start collecting coins.

## PASSING THE TORCH: MENTORING FUTURE LEGENDS

John J. Ford Jr. is a character whose influence and controversy in coin collecting and dealing throughout the 20th century has remained contentious. Walter Breen, an indomitable force in the 20th-century numismatic panorama, occupies a conspicuous niche in the field.

The intricate web of their affiliation unfurled its genesis in the late 1940s when Ford, in a prophetic stroke, recruited Breen to assume the mantle of researcher and cataloger for his burgeoning numismatic enterprise (Ford, 1993). Ford's discernment in recognizing Breen's innate talent and prodigious knowledge positioned him as a veritable beacon within the numismatic sphere, granting him unfettered access to the venerated repositories of coin collections and literary troves scattered across the nation. Ford's patronage was extremely generous, and he provided emotional and financial support for Breen during turbulent legal quagmires and personal tribulations.

In return, Breen regarded Ford with profound reverence, a sentiment nurtured by the wisdom and insight he gleaned from his mentor's guidance. Breen's contributions ranged from disseminating valuable insights and archival documentation pertaining to rare and historic coinage to pivotal involvement in some of the most iconic numismatic undertakings of Ford's career. These included, but are not limited to, the acquisition of the illustrious F.C.C. Boyd collection, the orchestrated disposition of the fabled Brasher Doubloon to the esteemed Mrs.

Norweb, the inception of the legendary Red Book, and the vigorous advocacy for California gold coinage (Ford, 1993).

Their shared ardor for numismatics, an effervescent flame that blazed brightly, defied the conventional boundaries separating professional and personal interests. One could detect an elusive but distinct thread of mirth and daring in their company. This quality orchestrated their participation in many numismatic escapades that have since become memorable chapters in the annals of numismatic chronicles.

The mentorship orchestrated by Ford and shared by Breen has etched its indomitable presence as one of the most consequential and influential chapters in the pages of numismatic history (Ford, 1993).

## FOSTERING THE NEXT GENERATION

I hold a sincere belief, an unwavering conviction, that numismatics transcends the boundaries of hobbyist pursuit or vocational engagement. It emerges as an all-encompassing passion, an ethereal thread that not only binds us to the tapestry of history, culture, and the sublime artistry encapsulated within every coin's alloyed embrace but electrifies our very souls with ecstasy! In this jubilant celebration of numismatic heritage, a clarion call resounds—one that shakes the heavens and the earth, imploring us to invest our collective energies in nurturing nascent leaders destined to shoulder this venerable legacy into an unknown future. This future glistens with the promise of numismatic wonderment!

This noble endeavor finds its roots in the realm of young numismatists, those intrepid souls who, with eager curiosity, dare to traverse the labyrinthine corridors of numismatic exploration. The dividends reaped from encouraging these youthful numismatists are, without a doubt, the most gratifying of all endeavors, like discovering a rare and ancient coin hidden in the sands of time.

In the numismatic milieu, knowledge reigns supreme, serving as the unwavering cornerstone upon which we construct the edifice of our shared passion. Thus, it becomes our duty to unfurl the banner of support for educational programs and initiatives, beckoning these initiates into the halls of numismatic enlightenment, where the secrets of coins are unveiled like treasures from a forgotten era.

Mentorship programs, a confluence of wisdom and aspiration, bestow guidance and the invaluable gift of reciprocal inspiration, a deeper appreciation for numismatics kindled within both mentor and mentee like a fire that burns brighter with every shared discovery.

I extend an open invitation to you, dear reader, to partake in our collective mission, to plunge headfirst into the sea of numismatic wisdom and swim alongside the giants of this field. Share your boundless insights, revelatory discoveries, and monumental achievements with our vibrant community of numismatic connoisseurs, for your voice is a gem, a priceless coin in our treasury. It matters not if you stand at the threshold of numismatic discovery or upon the pedestal of expert knowledge; your voice resonates with a unique value. I am so excited for you to create and share your story.

In numismatics, by leaving your mark, you enrich your understanding and ignite the fires of inspiration that lead others to follow in your footsteps. Together, let us embark on a transformative odyssey that renders numismatics more accessible, remarkably diverse, and thrillingly exhilarating for all who dare to embark upon this timeless quest. In it, every coin is a chapter, every collector a storyteller, and every moment an adventure.

## CASE STUDY: THE LEGENDARY COLLECTOR'S LEGACY

In a world where collectors abound, only one man can be said to have ascended to the rank of "The King of Coins"—Louis E. Eliasberg, Sr., a numismatic virtuoso whose legacy remains an enigma of passion, precision, and benevolence.

Born amidst the cobblestone streets of Baltimore, Maryland, in 1896, Eliasberg's destiny was already entwined with the glimmering allure of coins. A fortuitous inheritance of old coins from his father-in-law in 1925 kindled the spark of numismatic obsession within him (Bowers & Eliasberg, 1996).

Eliasberg spared no expense in his relentless pursuit of numismatic excellence. The rarest and most exquisite specimens were not beyond his reach, and he frequently set record prices at auctions and private acquisitions.

The "Eliasberg Specimen" of the 1913 Liberty Head nickel, acquired for a mere $3,750 in 1948, later commanded a staggering $5 million in a 2007 sale. The 1873-CC no-arrows Liberty Seated dime, purchased for $1,750 in 1950, fetched a remarkable $632,500 in 1996. And then, there was the legendary 1804 silver dollar, the "King of American Coins," acquired for $12,500 in 1945, which later changed hands for an astounding $1.815 million in 1997 (Bowers & Eliasberg, 1996).

Yet, Eliasberg was not content to be a solitary collector. He corresponded generously with fellow coin enthusiasts, sharing his insights and experiences and enriching the collective knowledge. In acknowledgment of his unparalleled achievement, Numismatic Gallery Magazine presented him with a special trophy.

In 1976, at 80, Eliasberg took his final leave from the realm of coins, leaving a legacy that would transcend generations. His collection, a priceless compendium of American numismatic history, passed into the care of his two children. The world gazed in awe as, in three historic auctions between 1982 and 1997, Eliasberg's trove was unveiled, its total value soaring past $50 million (Bowers & Eliasberg, 1996).

Louis E. Eliasberg, Sr. was more than a collector; he was a guardian of history, a curator of treasures, and an inspiration to coin enthusiasts worldwide. His journey through the labyrinth of numismatics, marked by unwavering dedication and unparalleled achievement, earned him the crown as the indisputable "King of Coins."

# BE PART OF THE LEGEND

Armed with this much information about the world you're exploring, you'll want to make sure other coin collectors are as well-versed as you are. Here's your chance!

Simply by sharing your honest opinion of this book and a little about your own collection, you'll point more beginners in the direction of the information they're looking for.

Thank you so much for your support. I wish you many triumphs as your journey continues.

# CONCLUSION: EMBARKING ON YOUR PROFOUND COIN-COLLECTING JOURNEY

You have reached the final chapter of this book; however, your coin-collecting adventure is far from over. You have now waded far into the fascinating world of numismatics.

You have looked into the wide range of collector coins, their financial potential, and the legends, techniques, and craftsmanship that went into their creation. You've even witnessed a real-life transformation from a hobbyist to a successful collector, armed with strategies you can apply to your very own collection.

There's an entire universe of wonder left to discover in coin collecting. Every coin you encounter has a tale to spin, a history to unveil, and a value to embrace. Every coin is a bridge to yesteryears, a mirror reflecting the essence of our contemporary world, and a harbinger of a future yet untold. These coins transcend mere metallic discs; they are living canvases of

166 | CONCLUSION: EMBARKING ON YOUR PROFOUND COIN-CO…

artistry, showcasing exquisite craftsmanship and emanating wellsprings of inspiration.

Coin collecting is more than just a hobby; it's a passionate adventure that allows you to express yourself, discover new things, and interact with a community of like-minded people. It is an investment in yourself, your future, and your legacy. It's a celebration of the sheer excitement that numismatics has to offer.

I hope this book has sparked a newfound interest in coin collecting or perhaps reignited your enthusiasm if you're already a seasoned collector. My goal was to present you with useful information, helpful hints, and valuable perspectives to help you grow and develop your collection. Above all, I hope it ignited that flame within you and inspired you to follow your personal dreams and goals.

As you set out on your own fulfilling and financially rewarding coin-collecting journey, remember this: It's about more than just amassing coins. It is about accumulating knowledge, making informed investments, and nurturing that deep-seated passion.

May your collections flourish, wisdom grow, and passion shine as brightly as the most coveted coins.

I wish you the best of luck in your numismatic pursuits!

# REFERENCES

*1941 penny value: Discover its worth.* CoinStudy. (2023, February 10). https://www.coinstudy.com/1941-penny-value.html

*2017 $25 fine silver coin: The Great Trail.* (n.d.). TSC. https://www.tsc.ca/pages/productdetails?nav=R%3A718551#:

*A comprehensive coin grading guide: How to value old coins yourself.* (n.d.). Warwick and Warwick. https://www.warwickandwarwick.com/news/guides/coin-grading-guide

*A modern Britannia – facing the future of Coin Design.* (n.d.). The Royal Mint. https://www.royalmint.com/britannia/britannia-2022/a-modern-britannia-facing-the-future-of-coin-design/

Anderson, S. (2022, December 16). *Coin Collection as a Long-Term Investment: The Pros and Cons.* Your Coffee Break. https://www.yourcoffeebreak.co.uk/money/26338797266/coin-collection-as-a-long-term-investment-the-pros-and-cons/#:

*The role of coins in history.* (2022, March 17). APMEX. https://learn.apmex.com/learning-guide/history/the-role-of-coins-in-history/

Aslpride. (2012, July 28). *What's different between contact Marks and hairlines?* Coin Talk. https://www.cointalk.com/threads/whats-different-between-contact-marks-and-hairlines.210714/

Associated Newspapers. (n.d.). *2019 news archive.* Daily Mail Online. https://i.dailymail.co.uk/1s/2019/12/05/17/21870770-7760683-image-a-6_1575568033935.jpg

Bank of Mexico. (n.d.). *Coin authenticity verification.* Coins authenticity verification. https://www.banxico.org.mx/banknotes-and-coins/coins-authenticity-verificati.html#saltos

BBC. (2013, April 26). *Rare liberty head nickel sells for $3.1m.* BBC News. https://www.bbc.com/news/world-us-canada-22314257

Bowers, Q. D., & Eliasberg, L. E. (1996). *Louis E. Eliasberg, sr.: King of coins.* Bowers and Merena Galleries.

Bretz, R. (2015, May 4). *Pedigrees & Hoards: The palace collection of Egypt's King Farouk.* CoinWeek. https://coinweek.com/pedigrees-hoards-the-palace-collection-of-egypts-king-farouk/

Bucki, J. (2021, February 26). *How to store your coin collection for future generations.* The Spruce Crafts. https://www.thesprucecrafts.com/how-to-safely-store-your-coins-768295

*Buy gold & silver bullion online: Free shipping.* JM Bullion. (2016, December 19). https://www.jmbullion.com/coin-info/us-silver-dollars/morgan-dollars/

*Buy gold & silver bullion online: Free shipping.* JM Bullion. (2023, June 22). https://www.jmbullion.com/6-gram-fiji-coca-cola-bottle-cap-silver-coin-varied/#:

Chen, J. (2023, July 31). *Troy ounce: Definition, history, and conversion table.* Investopedia. https://www.investopedia.com/terms/t/troyounce.asp#:

"CLASSIC NUMISMATIC QUOTES." The Numismatic Bibliomania Society (NBS). Last modified March 9, 2014. https://www.coinbooks.org/esylum_v17n10a11.html.

Coin collecting supplies. (n.d.). http://www.collectons.com/shop/lpc/142/Coin-Collecting-Supplies

*Coin Collection Market.* Transparency Market Research. (n.d.). https://www.transparencymarketresearch.com/coin-collecting-market.html

*Coin grading - how a coin grade translates to market value.* (2018, September 12). How Much Are My Coins Worth? https://howmucharemycoinsworth.com/6-pieces-that-make-coins-worth-money/coin-grading-how-a-coin-grade-translates-to-market-value/

Coins, A. in. (2023, June 27). *Unveiling the captivating world of contemporary coins by art in coins.* Medium. https://medium.com/@art_in_coins/unveiling-the-captivating-world-of-contemporary-coins-by-art-in-coins-404c6c9d51bd

Coreen. (2021, January 2). *What is the difference between the red and blue coin collecting books?* American Coin Stash. https://americancoinstash.com/2021/01/02/what-is-the-difference-between-the-red-and-blue-coin-collecting-books/#:

*Denarius of Brutus.* The Fitzwilliam Museum. (n.d.). https://fitzmuseum.cam.ac.uk/explore-our-collection/highlights/CM1474-1963

Encyclopædia Britannica, inc. (n.d.). *Origins of coins.* Encyclopædia Britannica. https://www.britannica.com/money/topic/coin/Origins-of-coins

FBI. (2021, September 9). *The FBI Warns the Public of Counterfeit Coin Scams.* Federal Bureau of Investigation. https://www.ic3.gov/Media/Y2021/PSA210909

*Five famous coin artists and their work.* (2022, May 24). APMEX. https://learn.

apmex.com/learning-guide/numismatics/five-famous-coin-artists-and-their-work-2/

Ford, J. (1993, January 1). *American numismatics: Perception vs. reality (part 1) : John J. Ford, jr..* Internet Archive. https://archive.org/details/JohnFord1993AnaPart1

*Free online coin cataloging software.* (n.d.). Numispace. https://numispace.com/

Garrett, J. (2022, December 29). *Jeff Garrett: Collecting Farouk.* NGC. https://www.ngccoin.com/news/article/11117/

Harmer, C. (2019, May 26). *How to choose the right metal detector? [step-by-step guide].* Detecting School. https://detectingschool.com/how-to-choose-a-metal-detector/

Harmer, C. (2023, April 23). *Efficient digging for successful detecting (A pro guide!).* Detecting School. https://detectingschool.com/how-to-dig-when-metal-detecting/#:

Hasson, N. (2016, June 10). *Archaeologists find ancient collector's hoard of Hasmonean coins.* Haaretz. https://www.haaretz.com/archaeology/2016-06-10/ty-article/archaeologists-find-hoard-of-hasmonean-coins/0000017f-dc8c-db5a-a57f-dceef4ec0000#:

Haughton, B. (2016, August 23). *The Roman Hoxne Hoard.* World History Encyclopedia. https://www.worldhistory.org/article/932/the-roman-hoxne-hoard/

Headley, S. (2022, January 19). *Get the inside scoop on buying and selling coins.* The Spruce Crafts. https://www.thesprucecrafts.com/tips-for-buying-and-selling-coins-768330

Headley, S. (2022, June 1). *Learn how to identify doubled die coins.* The Spruce Crafts. https://www.thesprucecrafts.com/doubled-die-coins-768451

Healey, M. (2014, May 19). *In coins, man found a century of learning.* The New York Times. https://www.nytimes.com/2014/05/19/us/in-coins-man-found-a-century-of-learning.html

Heller, P. (2023, January 19). *How to profit in numismatics.* Numismatic News. https://www.numismaticnews.net/coin-market/how-to-profit-in-numismatics

Holdefehr, K. (2023, May 31). *How to clean pennies and other older or collectible coins.* Real Simple. https://www.realsimple.com/home-organizing/cleaning/how-to-clean-coins

Holt, F. (2021, July 22). *When Money Talks: A History of Coins and Numismatics.* Oxford Academic. https://academic.oup.com/book/40033

Hornyak, T. (2011, April 11). *Canada's newest coin glows in the dark*. CNET. https://www.cnet.com/culture/canadas-newest-coin-glows-in-the-dark/

*How to determine rare coin values*. (n.d.). Numismatic Database. https://www.numiis.com/blog/how-to-determine-rare-coin-values/

*How to identify what coin you have*. (n.d.). Numismatic Database. https://www.numiis.com/blog/how-to-identify-what-coin-you-have/

*How to use a metal detector like a pro (extensive guide)*. (2022, March 8). Tech Metals Research. https://www.techmetalsresearch.com/guide/how-to-use-a-metal-detector/

How to work out the value of a coin. (n.d.). Bullion By Post. https://www.bullionbypost.co.uk/index/collectible-coins/coins-values/

James, R. (2020, April 13). *Security features on coins, currency, and bullion*. GovMint https://www.govmint.com/coin-authority/post/security-features-on-coins-currency-and-bullion

Jewers, C. (2020, November 16). *Gold coin showing British warrior Caratacus who led resistance against the Romans sells for £80,000*. Daily Mail Online. https://www.dailymail.co.uk/news/article-8956223/Gold-coin-showing-British-warrior-Caratacus-led-resistance-against-Romans-sells-80-000.html

Kelly, R. (2022, June 23). *What is numismatics? Meaning, qualifications, and example*. Investopedia. https://www.investopedia.com/terms/n/numismatics.asp#toc-understanding-numismatics

Khounani, A. (2021, November 10). *Jean Foy-Vaillant's arsacidarum imperium and achaemenidarum imperium*. Institute for the Study of the Ancient World. https://isaw.nyu.edu/library/blog/arsacidarum-imperium#:

Victor. (2015, June 3). *Petrarch and numismatics*. Late Roman bronze coins. https://www.lateromanbronzecoinforum.com/index.php?topic=725.0

Liberatore, S. (2022, December 9). *Pair of 165-year-old Levi Jeans pulled from a gold rush-era shipwreck sell for $114,000 at auction*. Daily Mail Online. https://www.dailymail.co.uk/sciencetech/article-11522469/Pair-165-year-old-Levi-jeans-pulled-Gold-Rush-era-shipwreck-sell-114-000-auction.html

*Louis Eliasberg - one of the world's most renowned numismatists*. (2021, July 1). Rare Coin Investments. https://southcapecoins.co.za/louis-eliasberg-one-of-the-worlds-most-renowned-numismatists/

Markowitz, M. (2022, February 6). *Let's get medieval: Collecting medieval coinage*. Coin Week. https://www.academia.edu/70589971/ Lets_Get_Medieval_Collecting_Medieval_Coinage

Maslar, D. A., Obaid, K., & Pukthuanthong, K. (2019, December 12). *U.S. coins market: Historical performance and anomalies*. SSRN. https://papers.ssrn.com/sol3/papers.cfm?abstract_id=3492347

MattG. (2023, May 19). *How to make money metal detecting coins in public places*. https://hobbylark.com/metal-detecting/How-to-Make-Money-Metal-Detecting-Coins-in-Public-Places

Meredith, S. (2020, May 6). *Design and selection process: How coins are made: U.S. Mint*. United States Mint. https://www.usmint.gov/news/inside-the-mint/how-coins-are-made-design-and-selection-process

MFEATeam. (2023, September 4). *Factors influencing the rarity and value of precious metal coins*. MFEA. https://www.mfea.com/factors-influencing-the-rarity-and-value-of-precious-metal-coins/

Millman, E. (2023, January 4). *Top 13 error coins worth money - price guide with pictures*. Gainesville Coins. https://www.gainesvillecoins.com/blog/error-coins-worth-money-guide

*Mongolian gobi bear*. Wildlife Protection – CIT Coin Invest AG. (n.d.). https://www.cit.li/collections/wildlifeprotection/#:

Nelson, J. (2023, February 28). *Is it a good idea to invest in rare coins?* Investopedia. https://www.investopedia.com/investing-in-rare-coins-5217604

Neuendorf, H. (2019, January 14). *A 16-year-old found a rare penny in his lunch money. then it sold for $204,000 at auction*. Artnet News. https://news.artnet.com/market/rare-1943-penny-auction-1436167

*Persian daric*. (n.d.). DBpedia. https://dbpedia.org/page/Persian_daric

*Reenactment for beginners: The A-Z guide to getting started with reenactment*. (n.d.). Living History archive. https://www.livinghistoryarchive.com/article/reenactment-for-beginners-the-a-z-guide-to-getting-started-with-reenactment#:

Rodger, J. (2019, July 5). *Two who discovered £3.3m Staffordshire Hoard at war 10 years on*. Birmingham Live. https://www.birminghammail.co.uk/news/midlands-news/two-men-who-discovered-33m-16535435

Sanders , M. (2021, February 28). *Mintmarks on United States coins*. American Numismatic Association. https://blog.money.org/coin-collecting/mint marks-on-united-states-coins

Sanders, M. (2022, January 17). *Coin design and engraving: Processes and person-*

*alities.* American Numismatic Association. https://blog.money.org/coin-collecting/coin-design-and-engraving

Seth, A. (2016, September 27). *Collecting coins. Why?.* LinkedIn. https://www.linkedin.com/pulse/collecting-coins-why-ajay-seth-the-collector-

Sherwood, H. (2022, March 2). *Rare "leopard" coin found by Norfolk detectorist expected to sell for £140,000.* The Guardian. https://www.theguardian.com/uk-news/2022/mar/02/rare-coin-unearthed-norfolk-reach-140000

Shutterly, M. (2023, March 28). *The dekadrachm – Athens' greatest coin.* CoinWeek. https://coinweek.com/the-dekadrachm-athens-greatest-coin/

StashTeam. (2023, June 14). *Short-term vs. long-term investing: A simplified guide.* Stash Learn. https://www.stash.com/learn/short-term-vs-long-term-investing/

Stevens, J. (2023, August 27). *Coinage in the Renaissance: A fascinating journey into history and artistry.* All My Treasures. https://allmytreasures.com/coinage-in-the-renaissance-a-fascinating-journey-into-history-and-artistry/

Sutevski, D. (2022, October 5). *Key factors that affect the value of collectible coins.* Entrepreneurship in a Box. https://www.entrepreneurshipinabox.com/19508/key-factors-that-affect-the-value-of-collectible-coins/

*Sylloge Nummorum Graecorum.* (n.d.). The British Academy. https://www.thebritishacademy.ac.uk/publishing/specialist-scholarly-publications/sylloge-nummorum-graecorum/

Texas Precious Metals. (2017, March 27). *Pattern coins: What they are and why they're special.* Texas Precious Metals. https://www.texmetals.com/news/pattern-coins-what-they-are-and-why-theyre-special/

*The art and significance of commemorative coins.* (2023, September 19). Coin Collecting. https://www.coincollecting.com/the-art-and-significance-of-commemorative-coins

The Coin Collector. (2019, August 28). *What are error coins?* 2 Clicks Coins. https://www.2-clicks-coins.com/article/what-is-an-error-coin-in-coin-collecting.html

*The most notable celebrity coin collectors .* (2023, April 4). Tavex Bullion. https://tavexbullion.co.uk/the-most-notable-celebrity-coin-collectors/

*The NGC coin grading system.* (n.d.). NGC. https://www.ngccoin.com/coin-grading/grading-process/ngc-grading-process.aspx

Woodford, C. (2023, September 1). *How metal detectors work.* Explain that Stuff. https://www.explainthatstuff.com/metaldetectors.html

*World coins: A journey through different cultures.* (2023, June 15). Coin Collecting. https://www.coincollecting.com/world-coins-a-journey-through-different-cultures

Yang, M. (2023, July 22). *Kentucky man finds "hoard" of Civil War gold coins worth millions in Cornfield.* The Guardian. https://www.theguardian.com/us-news/2023/jul/22/kentucky-man-digs-up-hoard-civil-war-gold-coins

Yeoman, R. S., Garrett, J., Bowers, Q. D., & Bressett, K. E. (2018). *A guide book of united states coins.* Whitman Publishing, LLC.

Young, D. (2022, March 9). *Amateur treasure Hunter unearths rare 14th-century gold coin.* Smithsonian. https://www.smithsonianmag.com/smart-news/amateur-treasure-hunter-unearths-rare-14th-century-gold-coin-180979703/

Zetlin, M. (2019, October 3). *People have been making up to $100,000 off 'coin hunting'-here's how the highly unusual Hobby Works.* CNBC. https://www.cnbc.com/2019/10/02/coin-roll-hunting-a-very-unusual-hobby-that-can-make-you-a-lot-of-money.html

Made in the USA
Coppell, TX
20 February 2024

29232614R00102